Unmasking Irresponsible Leadership

This book is unique given its scholarly angle in unmasking irresponsible leadership (IL) by focusing on its meaning. For the first time the concept of irresponsible leadership (IL) is explored in depth, the plethora of terms used in various disciplines is synthesised, and the ped-andragogy of teaching IL as a threshold concept of responsible leadership (RL) is discussed. The methodological approach adopted is creative and sound.

Following the call for business schools to do more in developing responsible leadership curriculum, the book is the first of its kind devoted to advocating a radical change in the management curriculum. It draws attention to the essence of developing a shared in-depth understanding of IL by addressing the misconceptions of theories and issues that have contributed to the epidemic corporate scandals worldwide. The authors provide a suite of reflective/reflexive tools for RL learning and development, including the first IL definitional framework useful for understanding IL perspectives. In addition the book is the first to introduce the ILRL board game, which increases the learner's flow state. Thus, the book highlights how various tools can be useful for engagement, and understanding curricula and ped-andragogical issues *vis-à-vis* corporate leadership practices and sustainability in turbulent times.

Our targeted audience: Academic researchers, final year undergraduates, and postgraduate (including Executive MBA) students and Higher Education Curricula developers/designers. The book provides many benefits, some of which include: Pertinent answers to important questions about responsible leadership and curriculum development; sophistication of qualitative research in management studies; in-depth understanding of irresponsible leadership from a cross-disciplinary perspective; support for leadership employability endeavours and equipping students with in-depth understanding of RL; assisting with developing reflective and reflexive practice; and in terms of ped-andragogy, encouraging innovation and creativity in teaching IL as a threshold concept of RL to reduce unnecessary management curricula bias.

Lola-Peach Martins is Senior Lecturer in HRM at Middlesex University, UK. She is leading Middlesex University's UN PRME (United Nations Principles for Responsible Management Education) Curriculum Development Project.

Maria De Lourdes Lazzarin is a researcher in Qualitative Social Research and holds a PhD in Management awarded by the University of Kent.

Principles for Responsible Management series
Editors:
Milenko Gudic, Carole Parkes, Patricia Flynn,
Kemi Ogunyemi, Amy Verbos

Since the inception of the UN-supported Principles for Responsible Management Education (PRME) in 2007, there has been increased debate over how to adapt management education to best meet the demands of the 21st-century business environment. While consensus has been reached by the majority of globally focused management education institutions that sustainability must be incorporated into management education curricula, the relevant question is no longer why management education should change, but how.

Volumes within the Routledge/PRME book series aim to cultivate and inspire actively engaged participants by offering practical examples and case studies to support the implementation of the Six Principles of Responsible Management Education. Books in the series aim to enable participants to transition from a global learning community to an action community.

Books in the series

Learning to Read the Signs
Reclaiming Pragmatism for the Practice of Sustainable Management, 2nd Edition
F. Byron (Ron) Nahser

Inspirational Guide for the Implementation of PRME
Placing Sustainability at the Heart of Management Education
Edited by the Principles for Responsible Management Education

Global Champions of Sustainable Development
Edited by Patricia M. Flynn, Milenko Gudic and Tay Keong Tana

Unmasking Irresponsible Leadership
Curriculum Development in 21st-Century Management Education
Lola-Peach Martins and Maria De Lourdes Lazzarin

Unmasking Irresponsible Leadership

Curriculum Development in
21st-Century Management Education

**Lola-Peach Martins and
Maria De Lourdes Lazzarin**

Routledge
Taylor & Francis Group

LONDON AND NEW YORK

First published 2020
by Routledge
2 Park Square, Milton Park, Abingdon, Oxon OX14 4RN

and by Routledge
52 Vanderbilt Avenue, New York, NY 10017

Routledge is an imprint of the Taylor & Francis Group, an informa business

British Library Cataloguing-in-Publication Data
A catalogue record for this book is available from the British Library

Library of Congress Cataloging-in-Publication Data
Names: Martins, Lola-Peach, author. | Lazzarin, Maria, author.
Title: Unmasking irresponsible leadership : curriculum development in
    21st century management education / Lola-Peach Martins and
    Maria Lazzarin.
Description: First Edition. | New York : Routledge, 2020. | Series:
    Principle for responsible management | Includes bibliographical
    references and index. |
Identifiers: LCCN 2019040047 (print) | LCCN 2019040048 (ebook) |
    ISBN 9780367367572 (hardback) | ISBN 9780429351228 (ebook)
Subjects: LCSH: Management—Study and teaching. | Business education.
Classification: LCC HD30.4 .M3697 2020 (print) | LCC HD30.4 (ebook) |
    DDC 658.0071/1—dc23
LC record available at https://lccn.loc.gov/2019040047
LC ebook record available at https://lccn.loc.gov/2019040048

ISBN: 978-0-367-36757-2 (hbk)
ISBN: 978-0-429-35122-8 (ebk)

Typeset in Times New Roman
by Apex CoVantage, LLC

To The Omnipotent, Omnipresent, and Omniscient

Contents

This book can be used for . . .

- Developing the management curricula and enriching student engagement in the area of RML, including leadership and management development (LMD);
- Teaching management students (including, MBAs/Executive MBAs) about the ontology of IL, including developing a shared understanding of IL as a threshold concept of RL;
- A potential tool to help prospective students choose business schools that have developed 21st-century management curricula, i.e. courses that teach IL as a threshold concept of RL. In this regard, the book targets a wide group of people including management consultants, management and leadership practitioners, and postgraduate management students who want to learn about holistic RL;
- Reflective practice in turbulent times, using the IL definitional framework and images and textbox features; and
- Learning about the sophistication of using NViVo for qualitative research in management studies, as well as for gaining in-depth understanding of IL from a cross-disciplinary perspective.

About the authors

Dr Lola-Peach Martins®, PhD, is a Senior Academician in HRM at Middlesex University, UK, where she also leads the UN PRME (United Nations Principles for Responsible Management Education) Irresponsible Leadership Curriculum Development Project. She has been responsible for the design and development of many leadership and management development courses, and collaborated with colleagues to design and develop Executive Leadership courses for various organisations including Middlesex University (London), SINOPEC (China), and Thailand MoD. Her PhD focused on the strategic management of managerial leaders, and distinguishing features of her thesis includes the history of the role of managerial leaders' (including [ir]responsible) behaviour from the early factory system of production to 21st century.

Dr Maria De Lourdes Lazzarin, PhD, is a researcher in Qualitative Social Research and holds a PhD in Management awarded by the University of Kent. The innovative and multi-disciplinary approach to the area of organisational justice and suppliers' relationships are distinguishing features of her thesis. Her current research focuses on organisational [in]justice, [ir]responsible leadership curriculum development, supply chain sustainability, and corporate social irresponsibility.

Acknowledgements

It would not have been possible to write this book without our contributors.

Professionals (including colleagues)

We would like to thank the following professionals for their support and contributions in various ways, particularly in the way that their studies have shaped our thinking, hence laying the foundation on which we have been able to build our work.

The Chartered Institute of Personnel and Development (CIPD) for keeping abreast of leadership, learning, and development matters to ensure members are continuously informed and keep up with professional standards; Professor Henry Mintzberg for his profound insight into the shortcomings of business schools *vis-à-vis* enhancing the quality of leadership in society; Professor J. Scott Armstrong for his insight on social irresponsibility; Professor Michael Brown for his insight on unethical leadership; Shawn O'Connor (Faculty Member, Harvard Business School) for his insight on the role and future of business schools in preparing leaders for ethical practices; Professor David Waldman for his insight on responsible leadership; Colonel Denise F. Williams for her insight on Toxic Leadership; Professor Craig Pearce for his insight on unethical executive behaviour; Dr Anthony Onwuegbuzie for his insight on what constitutes effective teaching; Professors Donald Lange and Nathan T. Washburn for their insight on behaviour in the context of corporate social responsibility/irresponsibility; and Professor Maria Rita D'Orsogna for her talk at Nottingham University which gave us much insight on corporate social irresponsibility in Italy (Oil Industry saga), and the amazing story she told about overcoming persecution and victimisation for advocating responsible leadership; Professor Carol Parkes, Dr Oliver Laasch, Dr Dirk Moosmayer, Dr Karen Blakeley, and Professor Roger N. Conaway, for their leadership on United Nations Global Compact initiative – the Principles for Responsible Management Education (PRME);

Professor Abby Ghobadian for his expertise in Strategic Management and Leadership; Dr Lisa Clarke for her NViVo Workshops; Professor Paul Hibbert and Professor Jill Brown for their peer review and feedback on journal manuscripts; we have considered much of the feedback offered, although not all are reflected in this book; Professor Clive Boddy for his insight on corporate psychopaths and Dr Joyanne De Four-Babb for her insight on pedagogy; and anyone else we have not mentioned here but have in one way or another assisted us along the way – a huge thanks to all.

Members of public-/private-sector organisations; research participants/respondents; professional development workshop participants

We would also like to thank all who have offered their help and have provided platforms for us to carry out research, disseminate our work, network with like-minds, and run professional development workshops: Middlesex University, The British Academy of Management (BAM), BAM Special Interest Groups (including colleagues associated with the United Nations Global Compact initiative – the Principles for Responsible Management Education (PRME), and the European School of Management and Technology (ESMT).

MDX students/graduates and guest lecturer

A very special thanks to all final year students/graduates that enrolled on the "Developing Leaders and Managers in Organisations" course at Middlesex University, London (class of 2015–2018), in particular those that participated in playing the *ILRL WordCloud Leadership Game*, and produced outstanding coursework that challenged our thinking of responsible leadership development; and Todd Roache, who delivered highly engaging Art-based Leadership and Management Development workshops with a particular focus on music and music making as a teaching method.

Anonymous

We are equally grateful to all who spoke to us anonymously about irresponsible leadership in the workplace; and for the publication of the CIPD 2019 Report "Rotten Apples, Bad Barrels, and Sticky Situations: An Evidence Review of Unethical Workplace Behaviour."

Family and friends

Thank you very much for your love and prayers.

Disclaimer

The cases presented here are compiled from published sources and are intended to be used as a basis for class/workshop discussions, rather than to effective or ineffective handing of any management situation.

Abbreviations

AC	After Christ
BAM	British Academy of Management
BD	Before Death
BIHECC	Business Industry and Higher Education Collaboration Council
BP	British Petroleum
CAQDAS	Computer-Assisted Qualitative Data Analysis Software
CEO	Chief Executive Officer
CIPD	Chartered Institute of Personnel and Development
CME	Critical Management Education
CPD	Continuous Professional Development
CSI	Corporate Social Irresponsibility
CSR	Corporate Social Responsibility
DTL	Dark Triad of Leadership
EMBA	Executive Master of Business Administration
HCBISC	House of Commons Business, Innovation and Skills Committee
HE	Higher Education
HEA	Higher Education Academy
HEI	Higher Education Institutions
HRD	Human Resource Development
HRM	Human Resource Management
IADA	Impulsive Aggressive Destructive Abusive
IL	Irresponsible Leadership
ILRL	Irresponsible Leadership Responsible Leadership
KUWASEP	Knowledge Understanding Wisdom Attitude Skill Emotion Perceived Self-Efficacy
LLD	Leadership Learning Development
LMD	Leadership and Management Development
MBA	Master of Business Administration
MNC	Multinational Corporations

PDW	Professional Development Workshop
PRME	Principles for Responsible Management Education
RL	Responsible Leadership
RM	Responsible Management
RML	Responsible Management Leadership
SI	Social Irresponsibility
SIG	Special Interest Group
SSCM	Sustainable Supply Chain Management
TEFs	Teacher Evaluation Forms
TL	Toxic Leadership
UK	United Kingdom
UL	Unethical Leadership
UN	United Nations
USA	United States of America
VW	Volkswagen

Part 1

Setting the scene for creating an IL definitional framework

1 Introduction

Why this book?

Building on many years of research, and the work of the United Nations Global Compact initiative – the Principles for Responsible Management Education (PRME), as well as participating in major conferences and special interest group (SIG) events,[1] we finally decided to focus our attention on developing a definitional framework[2] for irresponsible leadership (IL).[3] IL, in all ramifications of the term, is pertinent and various aspects of it have been of interest to us for many years. For example, the maltreatment of workers during the early factory system of production to 21st-century management practices such as injustice in global supply chains, all of which are known to have vast effects on various stakeholders and negative environmental and social impacts. Given the rise in corporate scandals and criticisms directed at business schools, we became interested in the responsible management education aspect, which has been at the heart of the United Nations (UN) Global Compact initiative – the PRME.

By writing this book we join the PRME, which also addresses the criticisms mentioned above. While it is clear that our book is not the first to rise to the challenge of addressing these criticisms, we hope that our work will find a way to positively contribute to the successes of our predecessors, colleagues, and the PRME, the message of which is conveyed in the *six principles*[4] below, and on which participating higher education institutions make a declaration:[5]

> **Principle 1 | Purpose**: We will develop the capabilities of students to be future generators of sustainable value for business and society at large and to work for an inclusive and sustainable global economy.
> **Principle 2 | Values**: We will incorporate into our academic activities, curricula, and organisational practices the values of global social

responsibility as portrayed in international initiatives such as the United Nations Global Compact.

Principle 3 | Method: We will create educational frameworks, materials, processes, and environments that enable effective learning experiences for responsible leadership.

Principle 4 | Research: We will engage in conceptual and empirical research that advances our understanding about the role, dynamics, and impact of corporations in the creation of sustainable social, environmental and economic value.

Principle 5 | Partnership: We will interact with managers of business corporations to extend our knowledge of their challenges in meeting social and environmental responsibilities and to explore jointly effective approaches to meeting these challenges.

Principle 6 | Dialogue: We will facilitate and support dialogue and debate among educators, students, business, government, consumers, media, civil society organisations, and other interested groups and stakeholders on critical issues related to global social responsibility and sustainability.

(PRME Secretariat, UN Global Compact, p. 12)

PRME leaders have relentlessly sought to address the criticisms against business schools in various ways, and have been at the heart of responsible management and responsible management education for over a decade. More recently they created a platform for a series of publications focusing on the subject. The book *Educating for Responsible Management: Putting Theory into Practice*, edited by Sunley and Leigh, more specifically, Chapter 2, written by Ross Hayes, Carole Parkes, and Alan Murray, draws attention to the PRME successes, and succinctly covers the history of responsible management education on a global scale. It draws attention to Manuel Escudero's 2006 paper in an engaging way. In his paper he outlined "a new vision for business schools to meet the changing demands of the decades to come." His work, and earlier work that we refer to in our book, emphasised the shortcomings of business schools, i.e. "failure of traditional approaches to be able to prepare graduates to respond to demands for a more responsible way of managing companies" (2017, p. 14). Furthermore, Hayes et al. provide useful information about working groups, regional chapters, relevant responsible management literature, and they provide a table highlighting the differences between traditional and responsible forms of management pedagogy. Another book titled *Responsible Business: The Textbook for Management Learning, Competence and Innovation* (2016) written by Laasch and Conaway, also PRME leaders (Laasch is Co-Founder of The Center for Responsible Management Education), also captured our attention. Their book also reflects Escudero's comment. That is, Laasch and Conaway suggested a competence based approach to teaching RL. They highlighted teaching responsible knowledge was insufficient and that "it does not lead to the type of resourceful and competent responsible manager we need to make the transition toward sustainable, responsible and ethical business happen." In this regard our book also focuses on IL pedandragogical matters, but in addition we draw specific attention to the essence of irresponsible leadership (IL) knowledge and meaning, which enhances responsible leadership[6] (RL) understanding. As advocates of critical and alternative approaches to LMD (Edward et al., 2013), we posit that such approaches are essential if students are going to effectively engage in learning about IL, and develop a shared understanding of the same.

In line with the PRME principles, we began to focus on responsible management and leadership (RML) curricula development, and became committed to writing a book about developing a definitional framework for teaching irresponsible leadership (IL), hence the focus on unmasking IL[7] as well as defining IL. This is also linked to our earlier research (which commenced over two decades ago) concerned with management and leadership behaviours and practices from pre-industrial revolution to the 21st-century era, organisational injustice, and supply chain management practices.

Regarding the management curricula, we observed an unnecessary bias on a global scale. More specifically it was clear to us that a considerably large amount of attention had been paid to RL in the management curricula without much attention given to IL. This has implications for continuous professional development (CPD) and life-long learning *vis-à-vis* RL behaviours and practices. Given the rise in the number of corporate scandals and the importance of thoroughly understanding what managers should do, and fundamentally should not do (Armstrong, 1977), we became passionate about developing management curricula and teaching IL as a threshold concept of RL. Adapting Meyer and Land's (2003) definition, in the context of education we define the "IL threshold concept" as *differentiating between IL and RL learning outcomes*[8] *so that IL can represent seeing RL in a new or clearly defined and holistic way, and pinpoint those factors that hinder such learning.* Continued rise in the number of corporate scandals is an indication that the concept of RL is centred around what Perkins (1999) described as "troublesome knowledge" (Perkins, 1999 in Meyer and Land, 2003, p. 1). Our study, which also involved in-depth critical analysis of these scandals, produced a plethora of terms used to describe leader behaviours and practices (including CEOs) linked with unethical and/or illegal practices. Furthermore, it soon became clear that neoliberalist/economist views have added to the confusion regarding the meaning of IL as a concept, and in terms of behaviour and practice, hence masking IL to portray it as something that is positive and sustainable. Also, despite the numerous terms used to describe the behaviours of leaders who fail to perform their leadership[9] role responsibly, this plethora of expressions had not been synthesised coherently, i.e. in such a way that could be useful for developing IL curriculum. In other words, until this publication there was no definitional framework, let alone an IL definition based on a synthesis of interdisciplinary discourse on leadership, business ethics, corporate social responsibility, and social responsibility. Therefore, this book has been written so that it can be used to support teaching IL as a threshold concept for gaining in-depth, shared understanding of RL. The definitional framework for teaching IL is based on the premise that understanding the meaning of IL and associated behaviours leading to IL practice can add clarity to the meaning of responsible leadership (RL), and hence impact management education and practice.

Overall, the four key motivations for writing this book are:

1   Our passion for the subject RL, hence research, teaching, learning, development, and practice in this regard;
2   The United Nations Global Compact and PRME Initiative and call for business schools to do more to improve responsible management education for sustainability, following the phenomenal increase of extremely costly corporate scandals particularly in the last decade;
3   The absence of a definitional framework for teaching IL as a threshold concept of RL;[10] and
4   The need to address unjustifiable management curricula bias (such bias suggests that intellectual integrity is compromised when ignored). According to Sadker and Sadker (2015, p. 1), curricula bias is concerned with how a body of knowledge is transmitted in business schools, i.e. "perpetuating only one interpretation of an issue, situation, or group of people. Such accounts simply distort complex issues by omitting different perspectives." For example, how the management curricula is designed and developed, what courses are on offer, how they have been selected, and how they are delivered.

Corporate scandals and the irresponsible leadership definitional dilemma

Irresponsible Leadership (IL) behaviours and practices in large corporations have been increasing at a phenomenal rate worldwide, costing the UK and USA billions in revenue per annum (Kirton, 2015; Gallup, 2013). Many authors have written about irresponsible behaviours and practices that have led to a significant number of environmental and social crises between 2008 and 2018. Banks for example, were held accountable for many of the social crises (Herzig and Moon, 2008). In fact, corporate scandals have been referred to as "one of the most important concerns of the management literature in the twenty-first century" (Pearce and Manz, 2011, p. 563), to the extent that scholars are studying whether regulatory interventions can pre-empt corporate misconduct (Hail et al., 2017).

Mounting evidence has revealed that many senior managers and CEOs of corporations (also see those mentioned below) refused to be account-able for any part played in social and environmental catastrophes. This draws particular attention to many issues amongst which is the lack of leadership competencies demonstrated in carrying out leadership duties responsibly (poor people management). The Investors in People Benchmark report (2017), Kirton (2015), and Gallup (2013) all drew explicit attention to the huge financial deficits associated with this problem. Literature on Ethics argues that the influence a leader has on an employee's unethical behaviour is linked to the managerial leader's responsible or irresponsible choice of behaviour (Casserley and Megginson, 2010). High profile cases, for example, Shell (Smith, 2010; also see cases in Endnotes),[11] open up a wide range of questions on unethicality, immorality, and unfairness (Ciulla, 2004; Rupp et al., 2015). Another high profile case is the 2013 collapse of the Rana Plaza building in Bangladesh that killed 1,100 factory workers (Greenhouse, 2013; Short et al., 2015). Another case, Kobe Steel, produced a "Mammoth report", which revealed the depth of safety breaches, resulting in the expulsion of the CEO and other senior executives' pay packets being slashed (Vaswani, 2018). Prior to this in 2017 the Samsung CEO was tried in court for bribery and a host of other corporate corruptions (Stone, et al., 2017). Samsung's case is particularly interesting as it drew attention to the issue of ethnic culture and its influence on corporate culture, hence how irresponsible behaviours and practices may be overshadowed by what may seem to be responsible from a loyalty perspective (for example, see Saadah's, 2017 study on the history of Samsung, South Korean culture, Chaebol,[12] Confucianism, and corporate governance).

Activity Area 1 Search for factual cases – read – reflect – conclude

Pertinent reports on corporate malpractices

Case Example: The House of Commons Business, Innovation and Skills Committee's (HCBISC) report (2016/17, pp. 26 and 29) revealed that Sports Direct, regarded as one of the [UK's] largest sports retail outlets, was established on a business model that supports disrespect towards most of its employees (p. 26). The report revealed that the CEO said that he did not know about the disgraceful management practices, which included turning a "blind eye" in order to maximise their profits. This type of unethical practice is regarded as "counter productive work behaviour" (Gifford et al., 2019), i.e. any type of behaviour or practice that violates or disrespects the organisations workforce.

Now find facts relating to:

Southern Health NHS Foundation's failure to probe more than 1,000 unexplained deaths

Caterpillar Incorporation's tax and accounting fraud case in 2016.

In some of the examples described in our book, some leaders appear to have accepted IL by directly using phrases such as "I am responsible" or "I take full responsibility" (see for example, HCBISC report, p. 24, and Matthey, 2018). Vaswanis (2018), in her article about Kobe's corruption, also drew attention to the tone of their report, which indicated that those responsible portrayed an attitude of contriteness and remorsefulness. However, from a critical perspective, we questioned whether this was an admission of IL.

Activity Area 2a Answer the question individually or in your group/team

What were the leaders (mentioned in Activity Area 1) really admitting to?

That they were unethical, incompetent, foolish, narcissistic, that their actions led various stakeholders into harm's way.

Activity 2b Answer the question individually or in your group/team

Search the internet for news about a recent corporate scandal – within the last two years. What terms would you use to describe the behaviour of managers/leaders held accountable?

Image 1.1 Stop Global Supply Chain Injustice

Image 1.2 Working Towards Responsible Supply Chain Management Around the
World
Source: Copyright © Maria De Lourdes Lazzarin 2019

A plethora of terms

The studies presented below give rise to similar questions about IL meaning. Greenberg and Baron (2008, p. 66) drew attention to the impact of the unethical behaviour of leaders. They argued that there are situational factors and organisational norms that encourage 'unethical' behaviour, and that the lack of managerial values may discourage integrity. Does the use of the term 'unethical' by Greenberg and Baron also mean 'irresponsible'? Other observations include corporate social responsibility (CSR) and leadership studies investigating sustainable supply chain management (SSCM), reporting on the same scandals. These studies also adopt the term unethical behaviour, which focuses on immorality, irresponsibility, and toxicity. Padilla et al. (2007, p. 177), in their paper "The Toxic Triangle: Destructive Leaders, Susceptible Followers, and Conducive Environments", draw attention to yet other adjective-nouns that raise similar questions. They stated that social scientists tended to avoid talking about the "dark side of leadership"; and while in more recent times this may not be the typical case, "destructive leadership" is defined in a somewhat nebulous way.

Our systematic review of the literature for this book revealed that a plethora of terms are adopted across disciplines when describing the actual behaviours and practices of those responsible for and/or involved in corporate scandals (also see Table 2.3). Yet to date the literature concerned with this dark side of leadership or IL continues to grow without a synthesised, coherent definitional framework for IL. Again, we questioned the following adjective-nouns such as "dark-side of leadership" and "destructive leadership", i.e. whether they have the same meaning as "irresponsible leadership."

Neoliberalist views of RL and IL practices, and criticism directed at business schools

Ghoshal's (2005) and Kanter's (2005) reviews on shareholder, stakeholder, and agency theories also uncover further complications associated with the meaning of IL, that is, the masking of IL through neoliberalist views of capitalism. The neoliberalist notion of the organisation's role or purpose contends that making profit to meet shareholder demands, no matter the cost to other stakeholders, is not an act of "social irresponsibility" (Armstrong, 1977; Kanter, 2005), even though such practices have led to unnecessarily harming others, and subsequently corporate scandals. Johnson (2009, 2018) posited that the lack of clarity between responsibility and irresponsibility makes abuse more likely within organisations. Thus, our literature review also focused on the neoliberalist-economist views that may have resulted in misconceptions of IL, as well as the disparity of terms used without drawing specific attention to IL.

Aside from the IL definitional dilemma, as mentioned in the beginning of the chapter, another motivation for writing this book is concerned with the significant criticisms directed at business schools *vis-à-vis* irresponsible management practices. Scholars such as Ghoshal (2005), Addison (2010), and Hall and Rowland (2016) posited that business schools contributed to leadership failures, and thus needed to take responsibility – address their own shortcomings. Hall and Rawland, while acknowledging that business schools have grown in number since 1965, state that vocational focus seems, by many, to have diminished. Ghoshal emphasised this by drawing attention to Mintzberg and Gosling (2002), who posited that business schools were failing at enhancing the quality of leadership, despite the phenomenal amount of research they carried out. Mintzberg's recent book *Bedtime Stories for Managers: Farewell Lofty Leadership, Welcome Engaging Management*, delivers a strong message by alluding to the need for a departure from bad management and leadership practices to "grounded engagement" (2019, p. 1).

Activity Area 3 Reflect and critically discuss

Criticism of business schools: failure

"Business schools produce enormous quantities of research. Yet they are failing in their fundamental purpose, which is to enhance the quality of leadership in society."

(Mintzberg, 2004b, p. 377)

Ghoshal (2005) argued that more action was required to ensure that failures in companies similar to Enron were prevented. Also, in an article published in 2015 by the Chartered Association of Business Schools, the author Suzy Jagger[13] drew attention to a number of related issues:

1   Ethics courses tended to be "dry and less than engaging"; and
2   Business schools need to offer a more holistic approach (both rule-based and values-based approaches) to teaching courses on ethics.

As highlighted above, there have been some other positive suggestions and developments. For example, former Forbes Business School contributor/ founder and former CEO of Stratus Prep, Shawn O'Connor, drew attention to the pertinent role business schools have in ensuring they do not contribute to the failures mentioned above. He strongly suggested that they should reflect on the extent to which they prepare management students for dealing with ethical questions they are likely to face post university (see Activity Area 4).

Activity Area 4 Reflect and critically discuss

Pertinent suggestion to business schools

"It is imperative that we ask ourselves if the world's leading business schools fully prepare MBA students for the ethical questions that these future business leaders will inevitably face in today's increasingly complex global corporate environment."

Shawn O'Connor, former Forbes business school contributor as well as founder and former CEO of Stratus Prep, one of the world's leading admissions counselling firms (October, 2018)

Our review of the literature further reveals that there has been emphasis on the importance of business ethics education, and that various educational bodies in the UK and abroad have strongly promoted responsible management. Examples include global, regional, and national initiatives such as:

- The PRME,[14] supported by a large number of universities and business schools
- National bodies such as QAA[15] (QAA, 2014 Education for Sustainable Development: Guidance for UK higher education providers, and QAA 2015, Subject Benchmark Statement)
- The CIPD[16] standards for human resource management (HRM) and human resource development (HRD), which encourage business schools to incorporate subjects of responsibility in management education
- The Higher Education Academy's (HEA) comprehensive report titled "Creating Cultures of Integrity" (Bell et al., 2014), which drew attention to a number of reports on the state of ethical education and guidance in the UK.

Evidence such as the number of core RL fields posed within management shows that business schools have recognised the essence of teaching RL for sustainability (Blowfield and Murray, 2011). However, Burchell et al.'s (2015) study, which focused on the changing nature of responsible education within UK business schools, revealed RL curricula needed significant improvement. Akin to this, Hibbert and Cunliffe (2015, p. 177) posited that there was a disconnect between RL knowledge and practice. They stated: "RL principles have to be supplemented by an engaged understanding of the responsibility of managers and leaders to actively challenge irresponsible practices." Thus, a key challenge corporate leaders need to confront is deciphering correctly between RL and IL (also see Chapter 9). This in itself is a leadership competency linked to strategic decision making, such as adopting a shareholder, stakeholder, or agency approach (Kanter, 2005).

According to the principle of non-contradiction, opposites cannot be right and wrong at the same time in the same respect (SEP,[17] 2015). We considered this generally held view in line with our research aim, which was to carry out research into developing management curricula in order to teach IL as a threshold concept of RL, hence assist with developing a shared in-depth understanding of IL through pedagogical/andragogical (or ped-andragogical) means. To fulfil the aim we asked two main question and set several objectives.

Questions

1 As educators, what else could we do to help future managers enhance their RL learning and development in turbulent times?
2 How might one go about developing IL curriculum?

Objectives – from an interdisciplinary perspective

- To determine the meaning of IL
- To identify the different terms and phrases used for IL
- To explore similarities and disparities between the way the terms and phrases are used
- To discuss ped-andragogical issues pertinent for IL curriculum development

The next chapter describes the methodological approach adopted for the study, which also addresses the dichotomy between IL and RL knowledge and practice.

Notes

1 The British Academy of Management's Sustainability and Responsible Management SIG, Responsible Leadership SIG, Leadership, Leadesrhip Learning and Development SIG, and the Executive Coaching Colloquium, ESMT Berlin.
2 We took an interdisciplinary approach (Leadership, Business Ethics, Corporate Social Responsibility, and Social Responsibility) for our research on creating an IL definitional framework.
3 IL adjective-noun, and in practice.
4 Used with the permission of Carol Parkes, PRME, Professional Development Workshop, British Academy of Management (BAM) 2017.
5 "As institutions of higher education involved in the development of current and future managers we declare our willingness to progress in the implementation, within our institution, of the following Principles, starting with those that are more relevant to our capacities and mission. We will report on progress to all our stakeholders and exchange effective practices related to these principles with other academic institutions:

> We understand that our own organisational practices should serve as example of the values and attitudes we convey to our students."

6 Maak and Pless (2006, p. 40) define responsible leadership as the art of building and sustaining good relationships to all relevant stakeholders. It is leadership that is not harmful to others. It is sometimes referred to as effective leadership. RL is about making business decisions next to the interests of the shareholders, and also takes into account all the other stakeholders for example employees, customers, clients, suppliers, the environment, the community, and future generations.
7 IL adjective-noun, and in practice.
8 (a) IL learning outcome: Students will be able to critically explain IL, clearly differentiate between RL and IL behaviours and practices; and challenge the IL status quo theoretically; and thus (b) RL learning outcome: Students will

be able to demonstrate in-depth understanding of RL through their knowledge and practice of RL, and thus provide evidence of CPD and employability in this regard.

9 We refer to leadership in the context a term used to the group of organisational leaders with core people management responsibilities (from junior managers to CEO levels).

10 RM and RL have been used interchangeably in the literature, therefore we adopt the term RL for consistency.

11 Case study examples of IL behaviours and practices:

Unitedhealth's overbilling scandal: www.reuters.com/article/us-unitedhealth-lawsuit/u-s-can-sue-unitedhealth-in-1-billion-medicare-case-judge-rules-idUSKCN1FX25S [Accessed 17/5/19].

Carillion's financial misrepresentation is reported to have led to pension losses and countless job losses: https://uk.reuters.com/article/us-carillion-collapse/carillion-bosses-personal-greed-and-recklessness-led-to-downfall-mps-idUKKCN1IG3GC [Accessed 17/5/19].

Mid Staffordshire NHS Trust health and safety breaches that led to deaths: www.theguardian.com/society/2015/oct/15/mid-staffs-nhs-trust-charged-over-deaths-of-four-patients [Accessed 17/5/19].

BP oil spillage scandal – string of events from data not being properly recorded to safety breaches: www.theguardian.com/environment/2016/dec/13/bp-near-misses-reveal-lack-safety-monitoring-refinery-oil-sites [Accessed 17/5/19].

Thames Water sewage leak scandal: www.theguardian.com/environment/2017/mar/22/thames-water-hit-with-record-fine-for-huge-sewage-leaks [Accessed 17/5/19].

VW emission scandal: www.bbc.co.uk/news/47937141 [Accessed 17/5/19].

Shell's oil pipes exposure and pollution scandal: www.amnesty.org.uk/press-releases/nigeria-long-awaited-victory-shell-finally-pays-out-%C2%A355-million-over-niger-delta-oil [Accessed 17/5/19].

Royal Manchester Hospital – dangerous short-staffing: www.google.co.uk/search?ei=HCrfXLqCIdPuxgO3tbHQCg&q=Royal+Manchester+Hospital+%E2%80%93+Dangerous+short-staffing.&oq=Royal+Manchester+Hospital+%E2%80%93+Dangerous+short-staffing.&gs_l=psy-ab.12 . . . 6173.9034.. 10787 . . . 0.0..0.124.219.2j1 . . . . . 0 . . . . 2j1..gws-wiz . . . . 0i71j33i160. ghSDdOppCAo [Accessed 17/5/19].

12 "Chaebol is a term used [that] refers to private corporations entirely controlled by family (Vaight, 2004 in Saadah, 2017).

13 *Principal Lecturer, University of Roehampton.*

14 Principles for Responsible Management Education.

15 Quality Assurance Agency for Higher Education http://eprints.uwe.ac.uk/23353/1/Education-sustainable-development-Guidance-June-14.pdf.

16 Chartered Institute of Personnel and Development.

17 Stanford Encyclopaedia of Philosophy (SEP); Aristotle's first, second, and third principles (or law) of non-contradiction, otherwise known as PNCs, have been debated amongst philosophers over the years and to date. There are three laws:

First – "It is impossible for the same thing to belong and not to belong at the same time to the same thing and in the same respect",

Second – "It is impossible to hold (suppose) the same thing to be and not to be",

Third – "Opposite assertions cannot be true at the same time" (SEP, 2015).

Bibliography

Addison, S., 2010, Business Schools Put Ethics High on MBA Agenda. *The Guardian*, 23 January 2010, Available at: www.theguardian.com/money/2010/jan/23/business-schools-ethics-mba [Accessed August 2010].

Armstrong, J. S., 1977, Social Irresponsibility in Management. *Journal of Business Research*, 5, 185–213.

Bell, E., Caulfield, P., Hibbert, P., & Jennings, P., 2014, *Creating Cultures of Integrity: Ethics Education in UK Business Schools*, UK: Higher Education Academy.

Blowfield, M. & Murray, A., 2011, *Corporate Responsibility*, 2nd Edition, Oxford: Oxford University Press.

Burchell, J., Kennedy, S., & Murray, A., 2015, Responsible Management Education in UK Business Schools: Critically Examining the Role of United Nations Principles for Responsible Management Education as a Driver for Change. *Management Learning*, 46:4, 479–497.

Casserley, T. & Megginson, D., 2010, A New Paradigm of Leadership Development. *Industrial and Commercial Training*, 42:6, 287–295.

Ciulla, J., 2004, Ethics and Leadership Effectiveness. In J. Antonakis, A. T. Cianciolo & R. J. Sternberg (Eds.), *The Nature of Leadership*, Thousand Oaks, CA: Sage Publications. 302–327.

CIPD – Chartered Institute of Personnel and Development, 2016/2017, Workday HR Outlook, Available at: www.cipd.co.uk/Images/hr-outlook_2017_tcm18-17697.pdf

CIPD – Chartered Institute of Personnel and Development, 2018, Labour Market Outlook, Available at: www.cipd.co.uk/Images/lmo-survey-summer2018_tcm18-45850.pdf

Edwards, G., Elliott, C., Izatt-White, M., & Schedlitzki, D., 2013, Critical and Alternative Approaches to Leadership Learning and Development. *Management Learning*, 44:1, 3–10, doi: 10.1177/1350507612473929

Gallup Report, 2013, State of the American Workplace, Gallup: USA, Available at: www.gallup.com/services/178514/state-american-workplace.aspx

Ghoshal, S., 2005, Bad Management Theories Are Destroying Good Management Practices. *Academy of Management Learning & Education*, 4:1, 75–91.

Gifford, J., Green, M., Barends, E., Janssen, B., Capezio, A., Ngo, P., & Nguyen, R., 2019, *Apples, Bad, Barrels, and Sticky Situations: An Evidence Review of Unethical Workplace Behaviour*, London: CIPD.

Greenberg, J. & Baron, R. A. (Eds.), 2008, *Behaviour in Organizations*, 9th Edition, Upper Saddle River, NJ: Pearson/Prentice Hall.

Greenhouse, S., 2013, Major Retailers Join Bangladesh Safety Plan. *The New York Times*, 13 May, Available at: www.nytimes.com/2013/05/14/business/global/hm-agrees-to-bangladesh-safety-plan.html

Hail, L., Tahoun, A., & Wang, C., 2017, *Corporate Scandals and Regulation, European Corporate Governance Institute (ECGI) – Law Working Paper No. 367/2017*, Available at: https://papers.ssrn.com/sol3/papers.cfm?abstract_id=2961535 [Accessed 25 May 2017].

Hall, R. D. & Rowland, C. A., 2016, Leadership Development for Managers in Turbulent Times. *Journal of Management Development*, 35:8, 942–955, https://doi.org/10.1108/JMD-09-2015-0121

Hayes, R., Parkes, C., & Murray, A., 2017, Development of Responsible Management Education and Principles of Responsible Management Education. In R. Sunley & J. Leigh (Eds.), *Educating for Responsible Management: Putting Theory into Practice*, London: Routledge.

Herzig, C., & Moon, J., 2013, Discourses on Corporate Social Ir/responsibility in the Financial Sector, *Journal Business Research*, 66, 1870–1880.

Hibbert, P. & Cunliffe, A., 2015, Responsible Management: Engaging Moral Reflexive Practice through Threshold Concepts. *Journal of Business Ethics*, 127:1, 177–188, https://doi.org/10.1007/s10551-013-1993-7

House of Commons Business, Innovation and Skills Committee Employment practices at Sports Direct Third Report of Session 2016–17, Available at: https://publications.parliament.uk/pa/cm201617/cmselect/cmbis/219/219.pdf

Investors in People, 2017, *People Management Benchmark: The Impact of Investing in People*, Available at: www.investorsinpeople.com/sites/default/files/2017_CIC_People_Management_Benchmark.pdf [Accessed 25 May 2018].

Jagger, S., 2015, *Rules and Values: Expectations for a Business Ethics Course*, Chartered Association for Business Schools, Available at: https://charteredabs.org/rules-and-values-expectations-for-a-business-ethics-course/

Johnson, C. E., 2009, *Meeting the Ethical Challenges of Leadership: Casting Light or Shadow*, Thousand Oaks, CA: Sage Publications.

Johnson, C. E., 2018, *Meeting the Ethical Challenges of Leadership: Casting Light or Shadow*, 6th Edition, London: Sage Publications.

Kanter, R., 2005, What Theories Do Audiences Want? Exploring the Demand Side. *Academy of Management Learning & Education*, 4:1, 93–95, Available at: www.jstor.org/stable/40214267

Kirton, H., 2015, *Poor Quality People Management Costs Employers £84 Billion a Year*. People Management, Chartered Institute of Personnel and Development, Available at: http://www2.cipd.co.uk/pm/peoplemanagement/b/weblog/archive/2015/09/10/poor-quality-people-management-costs-employers-163-84-billion-a-year.aspx

Laasch, O., & Conaway, R. N., 2016, *Responsible Business: The Textbook for Management Learning, Competence and Innovation*, 2nd Edition, Sheffield: Greenleaf.

Lin-Hi, N. & Blumberg, I., 2011, The Relationship between Corporate Governance, Global Governance, and Sustainable Profits: Lessons Learned from BP Corporate Governance. *The International Journal of Business in Society*, 11, 571–584.

Luo, Yadong, 2007, "Global Dimensions of Corporate Governance", Blackwell Publishing, p. 166.

Maak, T. & Pless, N. M., 2006, Responsible Leadership in a Stakeholder Society: A Relational Perspective. *Journal of Business Ethics*, 66, 99–115.

Matthey, J., 2018, Australia Is forgiving Steve Smith and Cameron Bancroft, But Why Not David Warner?. News.com.au, 2 April 2018, Available at: www.news.com.au/sport/cricket/australia-is-forgiving-steve-smith-and-cameron-bancroft-but-why-not-david-warner/news-story/0c6b856e8c03dc7b590cd8886ddb0fd9

Meyer, J. H. F. & Land, R., 2003, Threshold Concepts and Troublesome Knowledge: Linkages to Ways of Thinking and Practising within the Disciplines. In C. Rust (Ed.), *Improving Student Learning: Theory and Practice: Ten Years On*, Oxford:

OCSLD. 1–16, Available at: http://citeseerx.ist.psu.edu/viewdoc/download?doi= 10.1.1.476.3389&rep=rep1&type=pdf

Mintzberg, H., 2004a, Enough Leadership. *Harvard Business Review*, 82:11, 22.

Mintzberg, H., 2004b, *Managers Not MBAs: A Hard Look at the Soft Practice of Managing and Management Development*, San Francisco, CA: Berrett-Koehler Publishers.

Mintzberg, H., 2019, *Bedtime Stories for Managers: Farewell Lofty Leadership*, Oakland, CA: Berret-Koehler Publishers, Inc.

Mintzberg, H., & Gosling, J., 2002, Educating Managers Beyond Boarders. *Academy of Management Learning and Education*, 1:1, 64–76.

O'Connor, S., 2018, Former Forbes Business School Contributor: Founder and Former CEO of Stratus Prep, One of the World's Leading Admissions Counseling Firms. Personal communication via LinkedIn 20 October.

Padilla, A., Hogan, R., & Kaiser, R. B., 2007, The Toxic Triangle: Destructive Leaders, Susceptible Followers, and Conducive Environments. *The Leadership Quarterly*, 18, 176–194.

Pearce, C. L. & Manz, C. C., 2011, Leadership Centrality and Corporate Social Ir-Responsibility (CSIR): The Potential Ameliorating Effects of Self and Shared Leadership on CSIR. *Journal of Business Ethics*, 102, 563–579, DOI: 10.1007/s10551-011-0828-7

PRME Secretariat, UN Global Compact, after the Signature: A Guide to Engagement with the Principles for Responsible Management Education for New Signatories and Those New to PRME, 1-32, Available at: http://www.unprme.org/resource-docs/NewToPRMEToolkit.pdf [Accessed 1 June 2019].

QAA, 2014, Education for Sustainable Development: Guidance for UK higher education providers, Available at: http://eprints.uwe.ac.uk/23353/1/Education-sustainable-development-Guidance-June-14.pdf

QAA, 2015, Subject Benchmark Statement, Available at: http://qaa.ac.uk/./qaa/subject-benchmark-statements/sbs-business-management-15.pdf?sfvrsn=c7e1f781_10

Rupp, D. E., Wright, P. M., Aryee, S., & Luo, Y., 2015, Organizational Justice, Behavioral Ethics, and Corporate Social Responsibility: Finally the Three Shall Merge. *Management and Organization Review*, 11:1, 15–24.

Saadah, K., 2017, The Impact of Samsung Scandal in Corporate Culture in South Korean: Is Corporate Governance Necessary? *Journal Global & Strategies*, 11:2, http://dx.DOI.ORG/10.20473/jgs.11.2.2017.126.134

Sadker, D. & Sadker, M., 2015, Some Practical Ideas for Confronting Bias, Seven Forms of Bias in Instructional Materials, Available at: www.sadker.org/curricular-bias.html [Accessed 20 August 2015].

Short, J. L., Toffel, M. W., & Hugill, A. R., 2016, Monitoring Global Supply Chains. *Strategic Management Journal*, 37:9, 1878–1897, Available at: www.hbs.edu/faculty/Publication%20Files/ShortToffelHugill2016SMJ_4746e9b3-c482-4d09-b5aa-f2861fd1010f.pdf

Smith, D., 2010, Wiki Leaks Cables: Shell's Grip on Nigerian State Revealed. The Guardian, Available at: www.theguardian.com/business/2010/dec/08/wikileak-scablesshellnigeriaspying [Accessed 29 August 2015].

Stanford Encyclopaedia of Philosophy (SEP), 2015, Aristotle on Non-Contradiction, Available at: https://plato.stanford.edu/entries/aristotle-noncontradiction/ [Accessed 24 May 2015].

Stone, B., Kim, S., & King, I., 2017, Summer of SamSung: A Corruption Scandal, a Political Firestorm: And a Record Profit. *Bloomberg Businessweek*, Available at: www.bloomberg.com/news/features/2017-07-27/summer-of-samsung-a-corruption-scandal-a-political-firestorm-and-a-record-profit

Vaswani, K., 2018, Kobe Steel Scandal: How Did It Happen?, *BBC News Business*, Available at: www.bbc.co.uk/news/business-43298649 [Accessed 17 April 2019].

2 Creating an IL definitional framework

Research methodology

We based the research on the bricolage philosophy, which allows for ontological and epistemological flexibility due to its usefulness for investigating underresearched, yet pertinent issues. Ours is the first study to specifically investigate the idea of developing an IL definitional framework for teaching the subject as a threshold concept for understanding RL. However, it supports Hibbert and Cunliffe's (2015) work that focused on engaging students in moral reflexive practice by sensitising them in terms of ethical responsibilities, i.e. through threshold concepts (Meyer and Land, 2003). Furthermore, our work supports Lange and Washburn (2012) who suggested that CSR literature tended to focus on the meaning and expectations for responsible behaviour rather than irresponsible behaviour, despite the observers' reactions to bad behaviour. Whereas focusing on irresponsibility, they said, helps to explain CSR attributes in the observers mind.

The data gathering techniques for our study include article searches through multi-academic search engines to carry out a systematic literature review (academic and non-academic). We built on previous empirical research carried out individually or collaboratively between 1999 and 2015 (mentioned in Chapter 1) for triangulation purposes. These include a historical analysis of the role of managerial leaders, case studies, company documentation, semi-structured interviews, and professional development workshops using focus groups/semi-structured questionnaires. The studies drew attention to four critical issues pertinent to the more recent investigation towards the development of an IL definitional framework:

- The need to make clear that abusive nature of managerial leaders (IL) is rooted in social history, hence the essence of learning from history;
- The lack of management practitioners' understanding regarding their leadership role, hence the poor continuous professional development/ education in this field and the inevitable negative impact on performance;

- Problems management educators as well as students may encounter due to the lack of IL clarity, which is linked to poor learning; and
- The need to make clear the essence of deep learning *vis-à-vis* IL, which involves reflection and is paramount to dealing with ambiguities.

These points underpinned the research methodology adopted for our study, hence problematise the management curricula, conceptualise IL, and focus on the importance of learning about IL and associated issues. For example, Tsingos et al. (2015) suggested that there is a need to understand the learners' cognitive style/learning style and learning approach. In addition, they support the notion that reflection, which brings about clarity, plays an important role in the learner's learning. Brown and Mitchell (2010), referring to cognitive styles, posited that language ambiguity has advantages and disadvantages. For example, tolerance of ambiguity enables freedom to be innovative and creative, hence allowing for cognitive uncertainty. However, they pointed out that excessive tolerance of ambiguity can be detrimental. People can become incompetent by accepting every suggestion, not effectively subsuming necessary details and facts into their cognitive organisational structure. Therefore, too much tolerance (through, for example, rote learning, as opposed to deep learning; see Provitera and Esendal, 2008) is regarded as a barrier to effective learning – preventing meaningful considerations.

To further support the idea of creating an IL definitional framework for developing a shared, in-depth understanding of IL as a threshold concept of RL, we considered the essence of **content knowledge**. This is because of the way each of its components works in the production of meaning and experience of students in the educative process (Segall, 2004). Coe et al. (2014), referring to teacher effectiveness, identified six components that can be used to assess good quality teaching. Of the six, content knowledge appears first in the order of priority. According to Shulman (in Coe et al., 2014), content knowledge allows for the meaningful blending of content and ped-andragogy[1] for teaching. The research method and process is discussed next.

Activity Area 5 Reflect and critically discuss

Components of content knowledge

- Depth knowledge of the subjects being taught (for example, understanding through definitions, theories, concepts, provision of different perspectives)

- Being aware and understanding the ways students think about the content
- Demonstrating one's ability to evaluate the thinking behind students' own learning methods, and being able to identify students' common misconceptions

Research methods, process, and analysis

In 2015 we carried out a search of the literature around IL by adopting the 'Broad Search String' method. This involved using, for example, a number of clear search phrases, truncations, and synonyms (see Table 2.2). We took care to ensure inappropriate, strict limits did not exclude any valid search results. For example, no restrictions were placed on the date, as the purpose was to identify the extent to which the subject has been researched and published from a historical perspective – up to the 21st century. This method is said to work well for meta-analytical studies (Piper, 2013; Nasim et al., 2009). Qualitative meta-analysis is a quasi-statistical procedure, which involves using a large number of high quality studies (Timulak, 2009) for the synthetisation of data into a more coherent form. The search yielded a total of 8,882,200 hits (returned results) signifying that the subject is well researched. However, a modicum of this knowledge has been transferred to management curricula, hence creating undue bias in this regard. Whereas RL, which also yielded a significantly large number of hits (12,952,800), has been noticeably represented in the same curricula.

Next, a more specific search using vocabulary terms/categories/natural language was carried out (Bates et al., 1993) using eight IL phrases. The search phrases were restricted to those listed in Table 2.1 to narrow down the list to precise IL articles to ensure focus; however, no restrictions were placed on disciplines.

Table 2.1 Eight IL Phrases: Google Scholar

Leadership Phrase	Management Phrase
Irresponsible Leadership	Define Irresponsible Management
Irresponsible Leadership Definition	Irresponsible Manager
Define Irresponsible Leader	Irresponsible Management
Irresponsible Leader	
Comprehensive Definitional Framework For Irresponsible Leadership	

Table 2.2 Broad Search String IL and RL: Google Scholar, LP Martins et al., 2015

Leadership	Number of Hits	Leadership+	Number of Hits
1. Negative Leadership	2,490,000	1. Positive Leadership	2,650,000
2. Poor Leadership	2,470,000	2. Effective Leadership	2,610,000
3. Bad Leadership	2,000,000	3. Good Leadership	2,560,000
4. Dark Side of Leadership	528,000	4. Responsible Leadership	2,330,000
5. Destructive Leadership	338,000	5. Ethical Leadership	1,350,000
6. Evil Leadership	381,000	6. Spiritual Leadership	714,000
7. Ineffective Leadership	243,000	7. Productive	674,000
8. Toxic Leadership	94,900	8. Leadership	
9. Irresponsible Leadership	81,800	9. Constructive Leadership	315,000
10. Unethical Leadership	61,900	10. Authentic Leadership	313,000
11. Paralysed Leadership	31,700	11. Honest Leadership	275,000
12. Narcissistic Leadership	27,500	12. Accountable Leadership	267,000
13. Distrustful Leadership	26,100	13. Servant Leadership	264,000
14. Unaccountable Leadership	24,600	14. Transformational Leadership	180,000
15. Deceitful Leadership	21,500	15. Charismatic Leadership	140,000
16. Psychopathic Leadership	11,100	16. Trustful Leadership	13,800
17. Abusive Leadership	6,100		
TOTAL	**8,882,200**		**12,952,800**

The initial articles were used as a guide up till a point where substantial repetition occurred – taking into account breadth, depth, and current research of the subject (Hayton, 2015). This process enabled us to create mind maps, which was narrowed down to the final one (Figure 2.1). This final mind-map was converted into primary nodes (IL Sibling Nodes/Core IL Themes).

A literature review template consisting of five fields was developed in order to organise types of articles for the study. In the findings section of the template (consisting of Reference, Philosophical Stance, Method/Tool, Process, Strengths, Weaknesses, Other), concepts such as RL and ethical leadership were inversed (also see Activity Area 15), and antonyms checked – for example, adjectives such as "responsible" and "ethical" were checked for comparative analysis – to see whether they matched the terms used to describe "irresponsible behaviour" and practices in the IL specific literature.

Using a list of over 400 synonyms for the adjective "irresponsibility" from Thesaurus.Net, and the list of terms used to describe irresponsible leadership in Williams' (2005) study, the authors were able to explore the Core IL fields of literature using CAQDAS[2] (also see Table 2.3),[3] and to identify

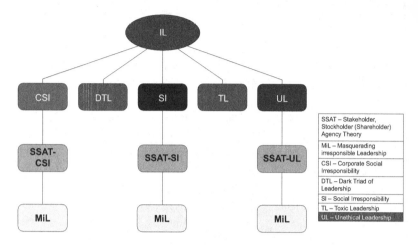

Figure 2.1 Final Literature Review Mind Map for Exploring the Meaning of IL

as well as decipher similarity, sameness, context, and meaning, and check rationality. The plethora of terms emerging from the literature was also used to explore how scholars and practitioners view and define the adjective-noun 'IL' and similar/associated adjective-nouns, for example UL, TL, and SI. The dichotomy between shareholder and stakeholder theories and the influence on management practice (IL) mentioned at the beginning of the book present a strong case for considering classical logic theory. According to McInerny (2005), classical logic regulates how people think into three acts of the mind: understanding, judgement, and reasoning.

Understanding is concerned with defining one's terms, what is thought about. For example, the former CEO of VW (Martin Winterkorn) was accused of being a deceitful and autocratic leader. Does this mean that he was an irresponsible leader? The literature review shows that unnecessary arguments can occur because two opponents use the same terms but may mean different things. Furthermore, according to Ixer (1999), assessing students on their abilities can be extremely problematic for educators if the meaning of terms are not clear. **Judgement** stems from an act of the mind, in that factual or truthful claims are made, which are either accepted or rejected. Terms, which are objects of one's thoughts, are meant to be defined first and then judgement about the terms stated. However, the need to seek definitional clarity regarding leadership has been contested in the academic literature (for example see Ciulla, 2004). **Reasoning** is concerned with establishing *why* judgments are true. For example, one should determine what warrants the claims made: establish the truthful basis on which one is placing the claims or beliefs, and check the degree to which the foundation of the claim or belief

Table 2.3 RM/RL Core Disciplines/Sub-fields/Core Fields also Embedded in Subfields/Key Theories[4]

Core Disciplines of RM/RL	Subfields within the Core Disciplines RM/RL	Core Fields also Embedded in the Subfields	Key IL Theories within the Core IL Fields (IL/SI/CSI/UL)
Leadership	• Leadership and management development (LMD) • Effective Leadership (EfL) • Responsible Leadership (RL) • Ethical Leadership (EL)	• Irresponsible Leadership (IL) • Unethical Leadership (UL) • Toxic Leadership (TL) • Dark Triad of Leadership (DTL)	Stakeholder Shareholder/ Stockholder Agency Theory
Business Ethics	• Ethical Leadership (EL) • Corporate Social Responsibility (CSR)	• Unethical Leadership (UL) • Corporate Social Irresponsibility (CSI) • Irresponsible leadership (IL) • Toxic Leadership (TL) • Dark Triad of leadership (DTL)	Stakeholder Shareholder/ Stockholder Agency Theory
Social Responsibility (SR)	• Ethical Leadership (EL) • Corporate Social Responsibility (CSR) • Management/ Leadership	• Social Irresponsibility (SI) • Unethical Leadership (UL) • Corporate Social Irresponsibility (CSI)	Stakeholder Shareholder/ Stockholder Agency Theory
Corporate Social Responsibility (CSR)	• Ethical Leadership (EL) • Social Responsibility (SR) • Management/ Leadership	• Social Irresponsibility (SI) • Unethical Leadership (UL) • Toxic Leadership (TL) • Corporate Social Irresponsibility (CSI) • Dark Triad of leadership (DTL)	Stakeholder Shareholder/ Stockholder Agency Theory

is solid? Thus, the question raised here is to what extent and how are management students informed about classical logic theory *vis-à-vis* IL? This has implications for the production of meaning and experience of students in the educative process, and after the course/in practice (Segall, 2004).

Overall, 70 research papers were uploaded to CAQDAS to begin in-depth analysis of the literature. The papers were also used to create the initial mind map (core themes around the main theme "IL").

CAQDAS literature-based (PDF) word frequency tests and cluster analysis were used to identify and compare key terms and issues, as well as organise and code emerging data from core IL fields. In addition, cluster analysis was used to determine relationships between variables, hence synthesise the IL meaning and perspectives. While this process enabled broad and in-depth comparisons to be made, as well as contextualisation of the data to gain further understanding of IL, it also shows the rootedness and complexity associated with defining IL.

In the next section the CAQDAS analytical results are reported and discussed *vis-à-vis* the core IL fields, which also provide a structure for the discussion.

Notes

1 The authors adopt the term ped-andragogy, which is pedagogy and andragogy combined to acknowledge the ongoing debate about a suitable term for the theory of adult learning. Hence, used here the authors concur with Knowles et al. (2005) on the essence of instructional and reflective teaching/learning methods *vis-à-vis* adult learners.
2 I.e. NViVo 11.
3 Core field = main discipline; Subfield = substantial body of literature within the core field; IL field = important body of literature within the subfield of RM/RL.
4 Core Disciplines considered for the study; Subfields: The substantial body of literature emerge from the Core Disciplines; Core IL Fields also embedded in subfields of the RM/EL literature.

Bibliography

Bates, M. J., Wilde, D. N., & Siegfried, S., 1993, An Analysis of Search Terminology Used by Humanities Scholars: The Getty Online Searching Project Report. *The Library Quarterly: Information, Community*, 63:1, 1–39, Available at: www.jstor.org/stable/4308771

Brown, M. E., & Mitchell, M. S., 2010, Ethical and Unethical Leadership: Exploring New Avenues for Future Research. *Business Ethics Quarterly*, 20:4, 583–616.

Ciulla, J., 2004, Ethics and Leadership Effectiveness. In J. Antonakis, A. T. Cianciolo & R. J. Sternberg (Eds.), *The Nature of Leadership*, Thousand Oaks, CA: Sage Publications. 302–327.

Coe, R., Aloisi, C., Higgins, S., & Major, L. E., 2014, *What Makes Great Teaching? Review of the Underpinning Research*, Available at: www.suttontrust.com/wp-content/uploads/2014/10/What-makes-great-teaching-FINAL-4.11.14.pdf

Hayton, J., 2015, *PhD: An Uncommon Guide to Research, Writing & PhD Life*, Available at: www.bookdepository.com/PhD-James-Hayton/9780993174100 [Accessed 7 September 2015].

Hibbert, P. & Cunliffe, A., 2015, Responsible Management: Engaging Moral Reflexive Practice Through Threshold Concepts. *Journal of Business Ethics*, 127:1, 177–188, https://doi.org/10.1007/s10551-013-1993-7.

Ixer, G., 1999, There's No Such Thing as Reflection. *The British Journal of Social Work*, 29:4, 513–527.

Knowles, M. S., Holton, E. F., & Swanson, R. A., 2005, *The Adult Learner: The Definitive Classic in Adult Education and Human Resource Development*, 6th Edition, Burlington, MA: Elsevier.

Lange, D. & Washburn, N. T., 2012, Understanding Attributions of Corporate Social Irresponsibility. *Academy of Management Review*, 37, 300–332.

Martins, L.-P., De Four-Babb, J., Lazzarin, M. D. L., Pawlik, J., & Yakovleva, N., 2015, Professional Development Workshop (PDW), Teaching Responsible Leadership in the Business Schools: Multi-Dimensional and Pedagogic Discussion. BAM conference at Portsmouth in association with University of Portsmouth, UK, 8–10 September.

McInerny, D. Q., 2005, *Being Logical: A Guide to Good Thinking*, New York: Random House. ix.

Meyer, J. H. F. & Land, R., 2003, Threshold Concepts and Troublesome Knowledge: Linkages to Ways of Thinking and Practising within the Disciplines. In C. Rust (Ed.), *Improving Student Learning: Theory and Practice: Ten Years On*. Oxford: OCSLD. 1–16, Available at: http://citeseerx.ist.psu.edu/viewdoc/download?doi=10.1.1.476.3389&rep=rep1&type=pdf

Nasim, S., Goff, P., & Tagg, C., 2009, Using Meta Analysis to Develop an Evidence Base to Inform Education Policy-Making. *Computer-Aided Qualitative Research*, 1–24.

Piper, R. J., 2013, *How to Write a Systematic Literature Review: A Guide for Medical Students, NSAMR*, University of Edinburgh, Available at: http://sites.cardiff.ac.uk/curesmed/files/2014/10/NSAMR-Systematic-Review.pdf [Accessed 18 April 2019].

Provitera, M. J. & Esendal, E., 2008, Learning and Teaching Styles in Management Education: Identifying, Analyzing, and Facilitating. *Journal of College Teaching & Learning*, 5:1, 69–78.

Segall, A., 2004, Revisiting Pedagogical Content Knowledge: The Pedagogy of Content/the Content of Pedagogy. *Teaching and Teacher Education*, 20, 489–504.

Thesaurus.net. Available at: www.thesaurus.net/irresponsible

Timulak, L., 2009, Meta-Analysis of Qualitative Studies: A Tool for Reviewing Qualitative Research Findings in Psychotherapy. *Psychotherapy Research*, 19:45, 591–600. DOI: 10.1080/10503300802477989

Tsingos, C., Bosnic-Anticevich, S., & Smith, L., 2015, Learning Styles and Approaches: Can Reflective Strategies Encourage Deep Learning? *Currents in Pharmacy Teaching and Learning*, 7:4, 492–504.

Williams, D. F., 2005, *Toxic Leadership in the U.S. Army*, USAWC Strategy Research Project, Available at: www.strategic studiesinstitute.army.mil/pdffiles/ksil3.pdf

Part 2

Contextualising IL

An interdisciplinary approach

3 Social Irresponsibility (SI), Corporate Social Irresponsibility (CSI), and Unethical Leadership (UL)

Armstrong (1977, p. 185) in his conceptual paper "Social Irresponsibility in Management", raised a pertinent point about the difficulty of defining social responsibility. In doing so he put forward the idea that there is a need to consider what a "manager should not do." It can be argued therefore that to address the meaning of social responsibility, it is important to define social irresponsibility (SI). Armstrong provided two SI definitions to create a better understanding of social responsibility, which made links to leadership behaviour that has a propensity towards harming others. He also introduced a second definition, the bias of which seems to lean towards shareholder theory highlighted in the first definition (see Activity Area 6).

Activity Area 6a Reflect and critically discuss

"A socially irresponsible act is a decision to accept an alternative that is thought by the decision maker to be inferior to another alternative when the effects upon all parties are considered. Generally this involves a gain by one party at the expense of the total system (shareholder/stockholder theory)."

". . . an act was irresponsible if a vast majority of unbiased observers would agree that this was so."

Activity Area 6b Study question and discuss

What are the implications of Armstrong's second SI definition for current IL studies, practices, and behaviour?

The two definitions depict the concerns relating to the theory of logical reasoning mentioned earlier in Chapter 2. Armstrong reported on an experiment concerned with determining whether the participants agreed with the first definition of SI reasoning. For the study, a convenience sample of 71 subjects was selected – these included faculty members, managers, and students. Using a self-administered questionnaire, the subjects were asked to "define a socially irresponsible act" using not more than 25 words. The variability in the responses was quite large, with approximately 12% of the subjects unable to provide any response, which may indicate an inability to view the concept logically (McInerny, 2005). Notwithstanding, 33% submitted definitions that were similar to the first definition. While it is a generally accepted one, some ambiguity regarding the meaning remained. Therefore, the second definition was used (Activity Area 6a).

Issues relating to the above definitions are reflected in the examples of well-known cases in the recent history of irresponsible leadership in multinational corporations. These cases (which occurred between 2010 and 2018) are linked to serious environmental issues and corporate scandals that harmed large numbers of people per event, depicting corporate social irresponsibility (CSI) and social irresponsibility (SI). CEOs of many of the corporations refused to accept any part played in the environmental and social crises and disasters. Hence, this raises questions about their understanding of SI/CSI.

Examples of IL cases provided at the beginning of the book also open up a wide range of similar questions about leadership reasoning behind unethical, immoral, and unfair behaviours. In 1958 Royal Dutch Shell began oil production in Nigeria's Niger Delta, however by the 1980s they were accused of being involved in money laundering (over £1.3bn) and major environmental and social havocs, which included oil spillages and unlawful positioning of pipelines. It was claimed at the time that growing evidence emerged *vis-à-vis* Shell's contribution to Nigeria's environmental deterioration (Abdulai, 2009; Smith, 2010), and that they were a primary cause of harm caused to hundreds of people. Many villagers were said to experience the devastation caused by reckless oil bunkering.[1] Yet, at the time it was claimed that Shell's senior leadership team refused to accept any part played in the irresponsibility saga, again raising questions about the comprehension of SI/CSI/UL practices.

The collapse of the Rana Plaza building in Bangladesh is another case that has been well documented. The building collapsed and killed 1,100 factory workers (Greenhouse, 2013; Short et al., 2016), causing immense harm to individuals, families, and small businesses. This incident involved the irresponsible behaviours of many leaders in supply chain management, making the investigation and onus of responsibility even more complex as several

Image 3.1 Defining SI

Image 3.2 IL Linked to Organisational Injustice

multinational corporations (MNCs) had been manufacturing products in the building. Besides losing sales and profits, the reputation of these MNCs was damaged as a result of the impact of harm caused by the collapse. These cases raise questions about immorality and injustice shown towards various stakeholders (including employees, consumers, and society), and highlight issues with neoliberalist-economist views. The neoliberalist-economist view favours and promotes profit-making at any cost, and is aimed at shareholders without due care and consideration of the negative impact on other stakeholders.

Typically, studies have shown that UL is clearly linked to SI and CSI, given that all three depict immoral behaviours directed towards others (as described above) whether external to and/or within the organisation (see for example Tepper et al., 2007). The SI definitions stated above, and the following UL and CSI definitions, provide a snapshot of the similarities between them. UL has been defined in the context of illegal behaviours that violate moral standards (see Activity Area 7).

Activity Area 7 Reflect and critically discuss

UL definition

> "Behaviors conducted and decisions made by organizational leaders that are illegal and/or violate moral standards, and those that impose processes and structures that promote unethical conduct by followers."
>
> Source: Brown and Mitchell (2010, p. 588)

Image 3.3 An Environmental Catastrophe: Crossing the Pipelines in Solidarity

Similarly, others have defined CSI in the context of behaviour which shows disregard, is extreme, and/or when personal gain at the expense of others is an objective (see Activity Area 8).

Activity Area 8 Reflect and critically discuss

CSI definition

> "Unethical executive behavior that shows disregard for the welfare of others, that at its extreme is manifested when executives seek personal gain at the expense of employees, shareholders and other organization stakeholders, and even society at large."
>
> Pearce and Manz (2011, p. 563)

It is clear from the three definitions (SI, CSI, UL) above that SI, CSI, and UL bear similarity in meaning (see Activity Area 9) to IL. We will explain this in more detail in Chapter 5, where we begin to discuss the meaning of IL in more depth.

Activity Area 9 Reflect and critically discuss

SI, CSI, UL definition similarities

- Leaders' behaviour
- Types of decisions/way decisions are made
- Unnecessary harm caused to other stakeholders
- Uncaring attitude

To draw further attention to the issue of meaning, the next section considers the term "leader" and what it means to lead others.

Who are leaders (all levels of management, including CEOs),[2] and what does it mean to lead others?

There have been a good number of attempts to define who leaders are and what they do (Gold et al., 2010; Day et al., 2009; Northhouse, 2015). Ciulla (2004, p. 312) states that "Just as a good leader has to be ethical and effective they also need be responsible and with some notion of the greatest good in mind" (see Activity Area 10 for brief distinctions between the terms and phrases "ethical", "effective", "responsible", and "the greatest good").

Activity Area 10 Reflect and critically discuss

Distinguishing between terms

- Ethical: Accepted principles of right or wrong that govern conduct
- Effective: Productive; impressive result
- Responsible: Ability to make decisions with little or no supervision
- The greatest good or *summum-bonum*: principles of goodness in which all moral values are included

Source: https://www.thefreedictionary.com/Responsible+Greatest+good

---

According to Maccoby (2007, in Ciulla, 2004, p. 314) narcissistic leaders believe that they are exceptions to the rule (also see DTL discussed below). Ciulla (1995) argued that a good leader needs to be both "ethical" and "effective" – the opposite being an unethical and ineffective leader. Furthermore, she put forward that several models of leadership portray the leader as "a saint" or "father-knows-best archetype": a person of perfection. Thus, the greatest ethical challenge for leaders stems from "the temptations to do evil and obligation to do good" (Ciulla, 2004, p. 322, also see definition of evil, p. 30). While other definitions of the term "leader" are respected, they will not be deliberated here. Instead, since the book focuses on clarifying IL, we select a definition that depicts both ends of the spectrum – irresponsibility and responsibility, or the positive and negative sides of the term "leader" (see Activity Area 11).

Activity Area 11 Reflect and critically discuss

Leader – what does this mean?

> "[A leader is a person who has an unusual power to create the conditions under which other people must live, move and have their being, conditions that can either be as illuminating as heaven or as shadowy as hell. A leader must take special responsibility for what's going on inside his or her own self, inside his or her own consciousness, lest the act of leadership create more harm than good]."
>
> Colle, Z., 2007 (in Johnson, 2009, p. 34)

It is worth taking a closer look at this dictum from the definition in Activity Area 11: To *"live, move, and have one's being [in a being with greater authority and power]."* It is a Christian dictum taken from the Book of Acts 17:28 in the Holy Bible.[3] Around AD 50, it is said that St Paul went to preach in Athens, which at the time was renowned for learning, philosophy, the fine arts, and immorality, including idol worshipping. St Paul had a partiality for the people of Athens, and laboured to teach them about the True Creator, i.e. to revere God alone. In a bid to identify with them he used the words of Epimendes, an ancient poet (c.600 BC), their own poet: "For in him we live and move and have our being." The words are about being totally dependent on God, *not* an image, a philosophy, or human hands. Thus, in the context of the discussion we present in our book, it is reasonable to assume that this means to have total faith in the leader as a being one that has full authority, and any action by the authoritative figure can be totally trusted – to be in the best interest of those being led, similar to the "Greatest Good" notion. Therefore, in this context, the leader is someone who has authority to create the condition under which those they are responsible for can thrive positively; and intrinsically the leader is trusted by those being led to create such conditions. In view of Colle's definition, it is possible to metaphorically identify two types of leaders, i.e. a leader that is as:

1   "Illuminating as heaven", which depicts a type of leader that is enlightening, helpful, informative, and offers guidance; or
2   "Shadowy as hell", which depicts a type of leader that is deceitful, misguiding, and destructive, therefore harmful.

People generally associate responsible behaviours with what is right, good, and moral, and in contrast, irresponsible behaviours are typically associated with being evil, wrong, harmful, bad, immoral, negative, or destructive. According to Johnson (2009 page 23; Activity Area 12), irresponsible leaders can be identified when preventive measures are ignored.

Activity Area 12   Reflect and critically discuss

Identifying irresponsible leadership

"[they fail to make responsible efforts to prevent followers' misdeeds, ignore or deny ethical problems, don't shoulder responsibility for the consequences of their directives, deny their duties to followers, or hold followers to higher standards than themselves]."

Activity Area 13 Reflect and critically discuss

Toxic leaders

". . . who possess the characteristic of irresponsibility refuse to answer for their actions." They have "reckless disregard for the costs of their actions to others as well as to themselves. . . . They see no need to do what is right, because they see no penalty for doing what is wrong. . . . A step beyond irresponsible is amoral. Leaders who are amoral are often also irresponsible and see themselves as outside the particular moral code. Not only will they not take responsibility for their actions, but their amorality "makes it nigh impossible for them to discern right from wrong".

Source: Williams, D.F., (Col), 2005, USAWC Toxic Leadership in the US Army, Strategy Research Project, Report, US Army (P3)

Williams (2005), on the other hand, looks at toxic Army officers, and characterises them as leaders who lack accountability, and have characteristics of irresponsibility since they refuse to answer to their actions as they do not think that there is a need to do the right things, and believe there is no penalty for wrongdoing – they see themselves outside the moral code of conduct (see Activity Area 13).

In organisational terms a leader's role is not always as straightforward. Typically, there are different types and levels of leaders with varying levels of authority, types of roles and tasks, styles, and attributes such as personalities (traits), perceptions, attitudes, beliefs, emotions,[4] and moral values. Since these factors and attributes are associated with how leaders enact their role, it is possible to use them to distinguish between leading responsibly and irresponsibly (see Williams, 2005). Furthermore, in Armstrong (1977), it is reported that some scholars do not see the leader's behaviour as irresponsible unless others are "seriously harmed" as a result of the act. Chapter 4's discourses help to contextualise harmful behaviour.

Notes

1 Exposed pipes and poor fracking equipment used by touts caused explosions and uncontrollable fires; villagers fled their homes, terrified and empty handed, to seek refuge elsewhere.
2 The term "leadership" is used in this book to refer to all levels of management, including CEOs.

3 Epimenides (c. 600 BC).
4 For example, the fear of losing one's job for non-compliance of orders, particularly where nepotism, favoritism, or cronyism have played a part in their recruitment selection (Babiak and Hare, 2006).

Bibliography

Abdulai, A. G., 2009, Are Multinational Corporations Compatible with Sustainable Development? The Experience of Developing Countries. In J. R. McIntyre, S. Ivanaj & V. Ivanaj (Eds.), *Multinational Enterprises and the Challenge of Sustainable Development*, Cheltenham, UK: Edward Elgar Publishing. 50–72.

Armstrong, J. S., 1977, Social Irresponsibility in Management. *Journal of Business Research*, 5, 185–213.

Babiak, P. & Hare, R. D., 2006, *Snakes in Suits: When Psychopaths Go to Work*, New York: HarperCollins.

Brown, M. E. & Mitchell, M. S., 2010, Ethical and Unethical Leadership: Exploring New Avenues for Future Research. *Business Ethics Quarterly*, 20:4, 583–616.

Ciulla, J. B., 1995, Leadership Ethics: Mapping the Territory. *Business Ethics Quarterly*, 5:1, 5–28.

Ciulla, J. B., 2004, Ethics and Leadership Effectiveness. In J. Antonakis, A. T. Cianciolo & R. J. Sternberg (Eds.), *The Nature of Leadership*, Thousand Oaks, CA: Sage Publications. 302–327.

Colle, Z., 2007, Evidence of Cover Up Kept to Tillman Hearings: The Sanfrancisco Chronicle, P.A1. In C. E. Johnson (Ed.), 2009, *Meeting the Ethical Challenges of Leadership*, London: Sage Publications. 34.

Day, D. V., Harrison, M. M., & Halpin, S. M., 2009, *An Integrative Approach to Leader Development: Connecting Adult Development, Identity and Expertise*, New York: Psychology Press Taylor Francis Group.

Gold, J., Thorpe, R., & Mumford, A., 2010, *Leadership and Management Development*, 5th Edition, London: Chartered Institute of Personnel and Development.

Greenhouse, S., 2013, Major Retailers Join Bangladesh Safety Plan. *The New York Times*, 13 May, Available at: www.nytimes.com/2013/05/14/business/global/hm-agrees-to-bangladesh-safety-plan.html

Johnson, C. E., 2009, *Meeting the Ethical Challenges of Leadership: Casting Light or Shadow*, Thousand Oaks, CA: Sage Publications.

Maccoby, M., 2007, *Narcissistic Leaders: Who Succeeds and Who Fails*, Boston, MA: Harvard Business School Press.

McInerny, D. Q., 2005, *Being Logical: A Guide to Good Thinking*, New York: Random House. ix.

Northhouse, P. G., 2015, *Leadership Theory and Practice*, 7th Edition, Thousand Oaks, CA: Sage Publications.

Pearce, C. L. & Manz, C. C., 2011, Leadership Centrality and Corporate Social Ir-Responsibility (CSIR): The Potential Ameliorating Effects of Self and Shared Leadership on CSIR. *Journal of Business Ethics*, 102, 563–579, DOI: 10.1007/s10551-011-0828-7

Short, J. L., Toffel, M. W., & Hugill, A. R., 2016, Monitoring Global Supply Chains. *Strategic Management Journal*, 37:9, 1878–1897, Available at: www.hbs.edu/faculty/Publication%20Files/ShortToffelHugill2016SMJ_4746e9b3-c482-4d09-b5aa-f2861fd1010f.pdf

Smith, D., 2010, Wiki Leaks Cables: Shell's Grip on Nigerian State Revealed. *The Guardian*, Available at: www.theguardian.com/business/2010/dec/08/wikileakscablesshellnigeriaspying [Accessed 29 August 2015].

Tepper, B. J., Moss, S. E., Lockhart, D. E., & Carr, J. C., 2007, Abusive Supervision, Upward Maintenance Communication, and Subordinates' Psychological Distress. *Academy of Management Journal*, 50, 1169–1180.

Williams, D. F., 2005, *Toxic Leadership in the U.S. Army: USAWC Strategy Research Project*, Available at: www.strategic studiesinstitute.army.mil/pdffiles/ksil3.pdf

4   Dark Triad of Leadership (DTL) and Toxic Leadership (TL)

Narcissism, Machiavellianism, and sub-clinical psychopathy

In view of the work of Jones and Figueredo (2013), Mathieu et al. (2014), Schyns and Schilling (2013), and Paulhus and Williams' (2002), it is clear that the behaviours exhibited by some leaders fall within the overlapping categories of the Dark Triad of Leadership – narcissism, Machiavellianism, and sub-clinical psychopathy. Likewise, these leadership conducts are categorised into what Mathieu et al. (2014) referred to as the common behaviours associated with the dark side of leadership, i.e. behaviours that are toxic, abusive, tyrannical, and destructive, and therefore harmful (Mathieu et al., 2014; Lipman-Blumen, 2005; Tepper, 2000; Ashforth, 1994; Einarsen et al., 2007).

Given the overlap between each of the behaviours exhibited by DTL type of leaders, in this chapter we focus on the work of Clive Boddy. Authors in the field of DTL whose work focuses on corporate psychopaths posit that DTL behaviours show a propensity towards a lack of emotional intelligence. Boddy (2011) also revealed that corporate psychopaths involved in bullying are about 1% of the population, and that they have long been confounded with criminality because of the way psychopathy has been conceptualised and studied. Therefore, he argued that corporate psychopaths tend to be leaders who appear to be more successful in the corporate environment. Similar to narcissists, corporate psychopaths are associated with CSI and SI because of their highly irresponsible behaviours and preoccupation with their own agenda and not with the well-being of anything or anyone else (Boddy, 2015). Boddy and other authors in the field of DTL have argued that corporate psychopaths are largely left to their own devices, perhaps because they are sometimes recruited by like-minds (Babiak and Hare, 2006). Hence, some organisations are renowned for leaving them unaccountable for their indiscretions rather

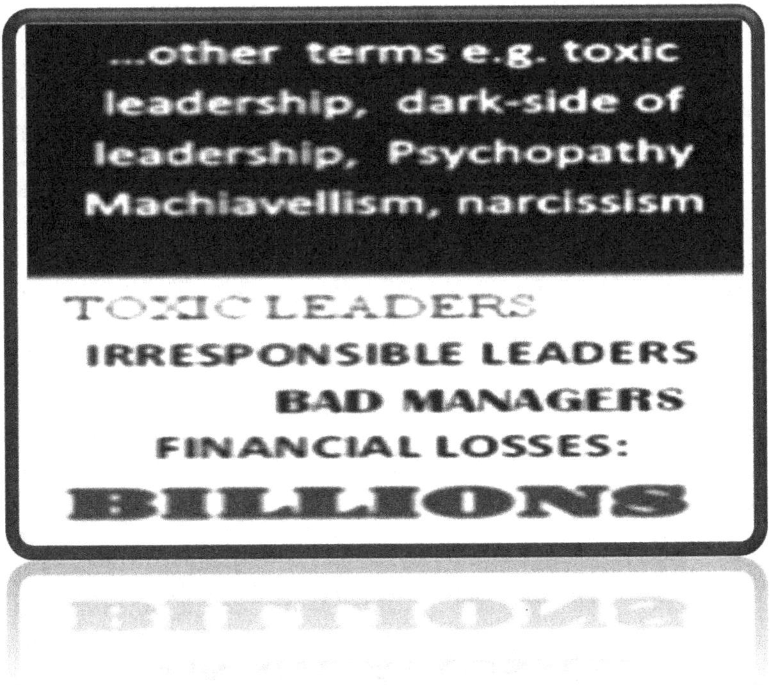

Image 4.1 Toxic Leaders . . . Billions

than ensuring that they carry out leadership duties responsibly. With little or no governance in terms of training and development and appropriate communication, psychopathic leaders have the tendency to cause unnecessary harm to the organisation. For example, employee career progression is negatively affected, employees become disheartened and directionless, and their personal and economic well-being is neglected, thus allowing harmful behaviours to manifest in leaps and bounds (Boddy, 2011). In this regard, Boddy has described the leadership style of corporate psychopaths as being irresponsible. Harmful conflict and abuse are rife under the leadership of corporate psychopaths and the organisational environment becomes toxic, unfriendly, and uncooperative (Ray and Jones, 2011). Some employees take revenge for their abuse by engaging in sabotage and workplace deviance; counter-productive work behaviour increases under DTL type of leaders (Boddy, 2015).

Image 4.2 It Has a Negative

In contrast to being trustworthy, by occupying leadership roles, DTL type of leaders claim capabilities and qualifications they do not really possess, and often elicit incompetent behaviours, leading to organisational scandals. They appropriate the good work of other employees and present it as their own output (Boddy, 2015). This type of fraudulent and incompetent behaviour demoralises employees at the receiving end of it. Furthermore, under the control of corporate psychopaths, decisions regarding core organisational functions are based on their personal dislikes and agendas and therefore outsourced, leading to the loss of internal expertise.

... Bad for Business

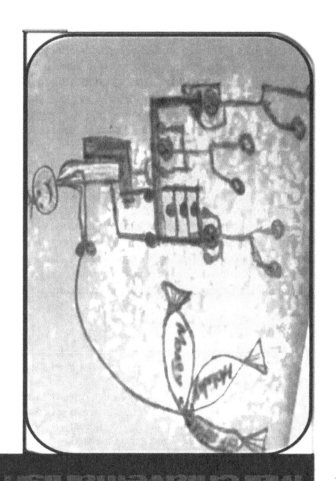

Machiavellianism...

Narcissism

Psychopathy

Image 4.3 ... Bad for Business

Source: Copyright © Lola-Peach Martins, 2019

Typically, environmental concerns are not shared by DTL types of leaders, which correlates with the reported willingness to engage in illegal toxic waste disposal (for example, see the case of Shell Nigeria discussed earlier) and lowered level of corporate social responsibility (Boddy, 2015). Responsible leadership at any level requires people management competencies (such as emotional intelligence), which studies have revealed many corporate leaders lack (CIPD, 2016, 2017; Gallup, 2013).

This lack of competencies leads to repeated misconducts and malpractices, hence creating distrustful cultures, which is a sign of the organisation's moral salience (Brown et al., 2016). Hence, the effect of abuse and irresponsibility on employees is that their job satisfaction severely declines (Sanecka, 2013, in Boddy, 2015) to the extent that among other work-related factors, the presence of managerial psychopathy is the single main determinant of job dissatisfaction (Boddy, 2017). Hence, one can conclude that the three "leadership" types in the Dark Triad (psychopathy, narcissism, and Machiavellianism) are irresponsible to the extent that, arguably, the former can be regarded as the most extreme form of IL. Furthermore, similar to Oplatka (2016, in Normore and Brooks, 2016), we conclude that narcissistic, egocentric, self-centered decision-making as well as poor regulation of emotions results in unethical climates, decreased well-being, and organisational failure.

Bibliography

Ashforth, B., 1994, Petty Tyranny in Organizations. *Human Relations*, 47, 755–778.

Babiak, P. & Hare, R. D., 2006, *Snakes in Suits: When Psychopaths Go to Work*, New York: HarperCollins.

Boddy, C. R., 2011, *Corporate Psychopaths*, London: Palgrave Macmillan.

Boddy, C. R., 2015, Organisational Psychopaths: A Ten Year Update. *Management Decision*, 53:10, 2407–2432, https://doi.org/10.1108/MD-04-2015-0114

Boddy, C. R., 2017, Psychopathic Leadership a Case Study of a Corporate Psychopath CEO. *Journal of Business Ethics*, 145, 41–156, DOI: 10.1007/s10551-015-2908-6

Brown, J. A., Dunn, P., & Buchholtz, A., 2016, The Role of Moral Salience in Firm-Stakeholder Repair. *Business Ethics Quarterly*, 26:2, 181–199.

CIPD – Chartered Institute of Personnel and Development, 2016/2017, Workday HR Outlook, Available at: www.cipd.co.uk/Images/hr-outlook_2017_tcm18-17697.pdf

Einarsen, S., Aasland, M. S., & Skogstad, A., 2007, Destructive Leadership Behaviour: A Definition and Conceptual Model. *Leadership Quarterly*, 18, 207–216.

Gallup Report, 2013, *State of the American Workplace, Gallup: USA*, Available at: www.gallup.com/services/178514/state-american-workplace.aspx

Jones, D. N. & Figueredo, A. J., 2013, The Core of darkness: Uncovering the Heart of the Dark Triad. *European Journal of Personality*, 27, 521–531.

Lipman-Blumen, J., 2005, *The Allure of Toxic Leaders: Why We Follow Destructive Bosses and Corrupt Politicians: And How We Can Survive Them*, Oxford: Oxford University Press.

Mathieu, C., Neumann, C. S., Hare, R. D., & Babiak, P., 2014, A Dark Side of Leadership: Corporate Psychopathy and Its Influence on Employee Well-Being and Job Satisfaction. *Personality and Individual Differences*, 59, 83–88.

Normore, A. H., & Brooks, J. S., 2016, *The Dark Side of Leadership: Identifying and Overcoming Unethical Practice in Organizations, Advances in Educational Administration*, Vol. 26, Bingley, UK: Emerald Group Publishing Limited.

Paulhus, D. L. & Williams, K. M., 2002, The Dark Triad of Personality: Narcissism, Machiavellianism, and Psychopathy. *Journal of Research in Personality*, 36, 556–563.

Ray, J. V. & Jones, S., 2011, Self-Reported Psychopathic Traits and Their Relation to Intentions to Engage in Environmental Offending. *International Journal of Offender Therapy and Comparative Criminology*, 55:3, 370–391.

Schyns, B., & Schilling, J., 2013, How Bad Are the Effects of Bad Leaders? A Meta-Analysis of Destructive Leadership and Its Outcomes. *The Leadership Quarterly*, 24:1, February, 138–158.

Tepper, B. J., 2000, Consequences of Abusive Supervision. *Academy of Management Journal*, 43, 178–190.

Tepper, B. J., Moss, S. E., Lockhart, D. E., & Carr, J. C., 2007, Abusive Supervision, Upward Maintenance Communication, and Subordinates' Psychological Distress. *Academy of Management Journal*, 50, 1169–1180.

5 Irresponsible leadership (IL)
Adjective-noun

General meaning of irresponsible and irresponsibility: Who's saying what?

Exploring the adjective-noun "irresponsible leadership" is similar to the study of "business ethics" (Wilson and McCalman, 2017). Here we begin to explore the meaning from a linguistic and general philosophical standpoint. There is no doubt that the terms irresponsible and irresponsibility allude to negativity – not being helpful or caring. Table 5.1 pays attention to some basic, yet pertinent, information from five dictionary/thesaurus sources,

Table 5.1 Adjective Source for 'Irresponsible'

Source	Meaning of Irresponsible/Irresposibility
Vocabulary.com	"Irresponsibility" is the quality of *not being trustworthy or dependable. Forgetting to pick your little brother up after school* [carelessness] would be evidence of your irresponsibility as a babysitter. . . . *Letting your house plants die [thoughtlessness], forgetting to walk your dog [thoughtlessness/carelessness],* or *leaving water boiling on the stove all afternoon* [carelessness] are all examples of irresponsibility. People who act in an irresponsible way have this *trait*.
	Both irresponsibility and irresponsible have the "not" prefix ir-, and responsible, originally a French word that first meant "legally accountable for one's actions", and later "trustworthy."
Quizlet.com	"irresponsible" – root word is "responsible"
Qa.answers.com **Master List of Morphemes**	"ir" is the prefix of "responsible" hence "ir" is an adjective -meaning "not"
Thesaurus.net	400+ synonyms for "irresponsible" https://www.thesaurus.net/irresponsible
MS Word Thesaurus	Irresponsible is an antonym (the opposite) of responsible

which provide a useful starting point for viewing IL from a conceptual perspective.

The scrabble board image (on page 48) represents a very basic meaning of leadership captured from the general body of leadership studies literature, which can be summarised as "leadership is about showing others the way", i.e. directing. However, it is well documented by scholars that the word "leadership" is a highly contested terrain, although not all agree that it is justly so (see for example, Ciulla, 2004). Many authors on leadership have said the disagreement stems from its complex nature, and thus it is difficult to define (Northhouse, 2015). Towards the end of the twentieth century Rost (1991, in Ciulla, 2004; see Table 5.2) provided a list of leadership definitions from a historical perspective, which given the similarities, may to some extent explain why Ciulla purported that focus should turn away from defining leadership. Rost's list might not provide an explicit single definition; however, for this book the list is useful for capturing what has been described as leadership actions/behaviours, which remain the same to date, and brings about some clarification regarding what they should/should not do (see Table 5.2).

Table 5.2 Leadership Actions/Behaviours Linked to Rost's List of Definitions, Adapted by L. Martins, 2018

Period	Key Leadership Adjectives	Action/Behavioural Description
1920s	Leadership ability	To impress the will of the leader on those led and induce obedience, respect, loyalty, and cooperation
1930s	Leadership as a process	Activities of many are organised to move in a specific direction by one
1940s	Leadership ability	Ability to persuade or direct men, apart from the prestige or power that comes from office or external circumstance
1950s	Leadership action	It is what leaders do in groups. The leader's authority is spontaneously accorded him by his fellow group members.
1960s	Leadership action/ behaviour	Actions by a person which influence other persons in a shared direction
1970s	Leadership action/ behaviour	Shows discretionary influence: behaviors under control of the leader which they may vary from individual to individual
1980s	Leadership action/ behaviour	Inspiring others to undertake some form of purposeful action as determined by the leader
1990s	Leadership relations	An influence relationship between leaders and followers who intend real changes that reflect their mutual purposes.

Northhouse (2015) and other authors also capture the fact that "leadership" is about relationship and influence. According to Northhouse (2015, p. 6), the definition of leadership in Activity Area 14 is an accepted and simple one.

Management and leadership scholars agree that leadership can be viewed as a role that involves social responsibility. In light of Stodghill's (1974) work, Northhouse posits that the term can be viewed from numerous perspectives (for example, position, trait, personality, power relationship, skills, authentic, spiritual, and process) with over 65 classification systems (Fleishman et al., 1971 in Northhouse, 2015). Ciulla (1995), on the other hand, pointed out that the ultimate question should not be "what is the definition of leadership" (p. 308), but about the best way to lead. She argues that trying to decipher meaning would not necessarily enhance understanding. While this comment may have some value, i.e. depending on various factors (for example, context, the nature of the learner, and the learning environment, to name only three), one cannot ignore the fact that the meaning of vocabulary is important (Mullins and Christy, 2013), as concepts can be misconstrued.

Activity Area 14 Reflect and critically discuss

Leadership definition

> "a process whereby an individual influences a group of individuals to achieve a common goal."

Belbin (see Mullins and Christy, 2013; Belbin, 1993) also argued that definitions matter quite significantly. Although Belbin was referring to distinguishing between teams and groups, while drawing attention to the use of vocabulary, he pointed out that the confusion [about] vocabulary should be addressed if principles [main beliefs of the concept] are to be retained" (Mullins and Christy, 2013, p. 272). For example, based on pure, unadulterated reasoning – what is good is right – ethical, and what is bad is wrong – unethical (Baker, 2011a). Regarding principles, there is no doubt that some management scholars view leadership as a positive force. Depending on the perspective of the term (positive or negative), a leader can be regarded as good when they can be trusted owing to qualities of conscientiousness (conscious of what is right and wrong, being careful, scrupulous, meticulous), and trustworthiness (being honest, dependable, loyal, credible). An evil leader on the other hand is the opposite (see Colle, 2007 in Johnson, 2009). For example, a leader cannot be trusted when systems fail woefully due to unethical business practices carried out by those senior business leaders responsible for the scandals referred to in Chapter 1 and the CIPD research report (Gifford et al., 2019).

Going back to Ciulla's comment on what the ultimate question should be, i.e. "what is the best way to lead?", we draw attention to Waldman and

Activity Area 15: Reflect and critically discuss

SOURCE	RL REASONING	IL QUESTIONING
Waldman, David A. &. Galvin, Benjamin M., 2008, Alternative Perspectives of Responsible Leadership, Organizational Dynamics, Vol. 37, No. 4, pp. 327–341, doi:10.1016	"A number of characterizations of exemplar leadership have been put forward in recent years. The existing lexicon of descriptors includes such terms as transformational, charismatic, authentic, ethical, participative, servant, shared, and even spiritual. So why introduce another term—responsible? We are not trying to reinvent the wheel of effective leadership here, and we acknowledge that each of the above characterizations has something to offer. At the same time, we also propose that the responsibility element is missing from these descriptors, and that it is actually this element that is at the heart of what effective leadership is all about. In a nutshell, to not be responsible is to not be effective as a leader."	In other words can we say to be ineffective is the same as being irresponsible i.e. if you are irresponsible you cannot be effective?
	"In everyday language, the term responsibility has several meanings, but they all revolve around the notion of controlling one's behaviour through internal mechanisms."	Therefore, can we say that to be irresponsible is to lack control over one's behaviour?
	"To be considered "responsible", an individual will need to feel an inner obligation to do the right thing toward others."	Can we say, to be irresponsible therefore is to not feel an inner obligation to do the right thing toward others?
	"We contend that responsible leadership is broader, more strategically oriented, and potentially less controversial than similar concepts, such as ethical leadership. For example, a focus on ethics can potentially get confused with values of particular religions and personal behavior on the part of a leader that may not affect others, while a focus on responsibility directs attention toward the particular others to whom a leader may be responsible. Thus, while responsibility is based on broad moral and/or legal standards, it is geared toward the specific concerns of others, an obligation to act on those standards, and to be accountable for the consequences of one's actions."	Therefore, can we say, irresponsibility is based on broad immoral and/or illegal standards; and that it is not geared toward the specific concerns of others; that it is where there is no obligation to act on those legal standards, and to be accountable for the consequences of one's actions.

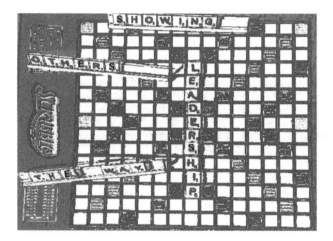

Image 5.1 Leadership: Showing Others the Way
Source: Copyright © Lola-Peach Martins, 2018

Galvin (2008), who indicate that the best way to lead is "responsibly." They provide a list of descriptors for effective leadership, i.e. transformational, charismatic, authentic, ethical, participative, servant, shared, and spiritual leadership. Then they introduce another descriptor, i.e. "responsible", claiming that each of the characterisations have something to offer, and in particular emphasise that the responsibility aspect of leadership is central to the meaning and activity of effective leadership. Therefore, taking another approach to unpacking the meaning of IL, we adopted an inversion technique, asking questions about IL in contrast to the responsibility descriptor and reasoning provided by Walman and Galvin (see Activity Area 15).

Negative forces: Evil, causing harm to others (intention to harm)

In view of ethical leadership, according to Johnson (2009), studies carried out by Palmer and Jung draw attention to the need to manage negative forces, but in order to do so it must first be admitted that they exist. As Colle (2007) suggests, there are two sides of leadership, good and evil, which can have a positive or negative effect on followers, and many studies involving SI, ethics, and CSR confirms this view. No matter what level of authority and task is required for the role, the two sides to leadership suggest that there is a choice to lead responsibly or irresponsibly. That said, it is possible that the choice is not always thoroughly considered before decisions are made. Notwithstanding, the fact remains that if a leader decides to act, or simply behave irresponsibly, the power and influence wielded has the propensity to cause harm, hence destroy, as evidenced in the case studies highlighted earlier (see Activity Area 1, Chapter 1, for a snapshot of examples).

The question of whether the person occupying the role of a leader is good or evil is somewhat complex. For example, such persons may be deemed good/effective by taking actions that yield profits at whatever cost (neoliberalist/economist view of leadership). In this regard some writers regard destructive leadership as an oxymoron (Padilla et al., 2007).

Padilla et al.'s view can best be expressed through a quote highlighted by Alvesson and Spicer (2012, p. 369). See Activity Area 16.

Drawing from stakeholder theory, which defines leadership from a position perspective (Armstrong, 1977), it is said that leadership is the position held by a leader, hence the capacity to lead without deciding to favour one group out of selfish interest as this typically involves the neglect of other groups that are likely to be unnecessarily harmed as a result. This "position" viewpoint is useful for the current study as it is quite broad and when viewed critically resonates with other leadership definitions that focus on trait, personality, power relationship, skills, authenticity, spirituality, and process.

Activity Area 16 Reflect and critically discuss

Confusion and vagueness of leadership

> "There is notoriously little agreement about how exactly we might define leadership. Two-thirds of leadership texts do not define the subject, while the other third tend to provide quite different definitions. Our impression is that this has not changed much in recent years and that the increasing popularity of using the idea of leadership has reinforced conceptual confusion and endemic vagueness."

Source: Alvesson and Spicer (2012, p. 369)

It is quite clear that there is a plethora of terms used in the literature to explain IL. However, Armstrong (1977) makes it clear that IL is unequivocally linked to harmfulness.[1] He posits that it is better to consider what a manager should not do rather than focus on what a manager should do. Thus,

Image 5.2 Trust

his definition (above) draws attention to the issue of harming others, and the need to distinguish between IL and RL.

A review of stockholder theory makes it clear that it is likely the typical manager is expected to harm others in carrying out their managerial duties (Armstrong, 1977). This idea raises serious questions about how leaders are recruited (Babiak and Hare, 2006) and issues around their training, learning, and development, given that harm is typically associated with the term "evil."

Zimbardo (2008, Kindle Edition) defines evil from a psychological viewpoint, i.e. as intentional negative behaviour (see Activity Area 17). He acknowledges that his definition draws attention to a person or people knowing to do better; however, they choose to do worse. What if the perpetrator does not know any better? According to Johnson, (2009, 2018), failing to make reasonable efforts to prevent harm is an act of irresponsibility, and evil leaders commit atrocities, such as those listed in Zimbardo's definition of evil.

The harm caused may be obvious, however, according to Armstrong (1977) and Johnson (2009, 2018), it is not always easy to distinguish IL from RL in practice. Furthermore, without a shared in-depth understanding approach it is not always clear when IL actually occurs (for example see Table 5.3) as the quotes and questions derived from the work of Drucker (1973) serves to demonstrate.

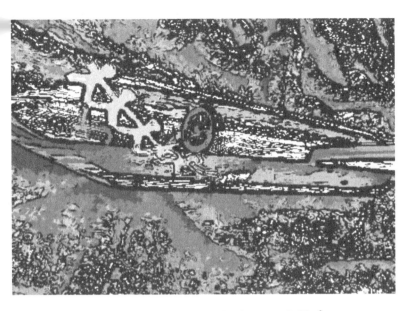

Image 5.3 Leading Irresponsibly: Over the Edge into Harm's Way[2]
Source: Copyright © Maria De Lourdes Lazzarin, 2019

Activity Area 17 Reflect and critically discuss

Definition of evil

Key words Zimbardo uses in his definition are as follows:

- Intentional behaviour
- Causing harm
- Abuse
- Actions that are demeaning
- Actions that dehumanise
- Actions that destroy innocent others
- Eliciting others to carry out any of the above i.e. generally using one's authority and power to encourage these wicked actions on one's behalf

Source: Zimbardo, 2008, Kindle Edition

Image 5.4 Leading Responsibly: Safety, Protection, and Well-being[3]
Source: Maria de Lourdes Lazzarin, 2019

Williams' (2005) study on Toxic Leadership in the US Army also found that typically IL tends to be associated with evil and harmful behaviour – whether intentional or non-intentional. Given the interdisciplinary nature of leadership and the oxymoronic nature of irresponsible leadership, IL must be understood in context to simplify any potential complexity. For example, according to shareholder theory, a chief executive officer (CEO) focused on maximising profit for the benefit of the stockholder at the expense of harming other interest groups is a "leader" who has not acted irresponsibly. However, if such behaviour is challenged, where a majority of interest groups raise a complaint, the behaviour might be considered harmful (Armstrong, 1977). Problems in challenging favouritism can be made difficult in countries where such practices are backed by corrupt governments and legal systems. Stockholder theory suggests that to meet the demands of the stockholders (typically the majority shareholder), harming other stakeholders [typically employees] is inevitable if profits are to be maximised (Demacarty, 2009). However, Dermacarty's study also shows that similar high profits can be generated through responsible leadership (RL), i.e. leadership that is not unnecessarily harmful to others. Drawing attention to these

Table 5.3 Paraphrasing IL, by L.P. Martins, 2018, Based on Quotes by Drucker

(Drucker, 1973, p. 239)	*"A university which fails to prepare tomorrow's leaders and professionals is not socially responsible, no matter how many 'good works' it engages in . . ."*	Does this mean that there is correlation between a university that fails to facilitate the learning and development of students, and IL? Is social irresponsibility an indicator of IL?
(Drucker, 1973, p. 240)	*"The manager is duty-bound to preserve the performance capacity of the institution in his care. To jeopardise it, no matter how noble the motive, is irresponsibility. These institutions too are capital assets of society on the performance of which society depends."*	Does this mean that the manager that does not feel obliged to preserve the performance capacity of the institution in his care is an irresponsible leader?
(Drucker, 1973, p. 212)	*"A responsible work force does indeed make very high demands on managers. It demands that they be truly competent – and competent as managers rather than as psychologists or psychotherapists. It demands that they take their own work seriously. It demands that they themselves take responsibility for their jobs and their performances. . . . To demand it of others without demanding it of oneself is futile and irresponsible."*	Does this mean that managers that fail to lead by example are incompetent? Are incompetent leaders, irresponsible leaders?
(Drucker, 1973, p. 64)	*"To wait until a business – or an industry – is in trouble is playing Russian roulette. It is irresponsible management."*	Does irresponsible management mean IL? Are non-proactive managers irresponsible leaders?

distinctions makes it possible to understand the essence of addressing the problems associated IL meaning, hence the need to create a definitional framework and develop a shared in-depth understanding of IL.

The following two chapters provide an analysis of our research findings generated through the CAQDAS. We also discuss the process of our analysis, and conclude with an IL definitional framework for teaching IL as a threshold concept of RL.

Stockholder/Shareholder Theory
Money! Money! Money! Money!
Whatever the cost!!!

Image 5.5 Stockholder/Shareholder Theory: Money! Money! Money! Money!
Whatever the Cost!!!

Notes

1 Deliberate harmful behaviour (Armstrong, 1977), Toxic Leadership, corporate psychopaths (Babiak and Hare, 2006; Boddy, 2011), negative side of leadership, destructive leadership, narcissistic leadership, and abusive supervision (Maccoby, 2007; Harris et al., 2013).
2 Boat created by Matthew Lazzarin De Morais.
3 Boat created by Matthew Lazzarin De Morais.

Bibliography

Alvesson, M. & Spicer, A., 2012, Critical Leadership Studies: The Case for Critical Performativity. *Human Relations*, 65:3, 367–390.

Armstrong, J. S., 1977, Social Irresponsibility in Management. *Journal of Business Research*, 5, 185–213.

Babiak, P. & Hare, R. D., 2006, *Snakes in Suits: When Psychopaths Go to Work*, New York: HarperCollins.

Baker, M., 2011a, *In Other Words: A Coursebook on Translation*, London: Routledge Taylor and Francis.

Belbin, R. M., 1993, *Team Roles at Work*, Oxford: Butterworth-Heinemann.

Boddy, C. R., 2011, *Corporate Psychopaths*, London: Palgrave Macmillan.

Ciulla, J. B., 1995, Leadership Ethics: Mapping the Territory. *Business Ethics Quarterly*, 5:1, 5–28.

Ciulla, J. B., 2004, Ethics and Leadership Effectiveness. In J. Antonakis, A. T. Cianciolo & R. J. Sternberg (Eds.), *The Nature of Leadership*, Thousand Oaks, CA: Sage Publications. 302–327.

Colle, Z., 2007, Evidence of Cover Up Kept to Tillman Hearings: The Sanfrancisco Chronicle, P.A1. In C. E. Johnson (Ed.), 2009, *Meeting the Ethical Challenges of Leadership*, London: Sage Publications. 34.

Demacarty, P., 2009, Financial Returns of Corporate Social Responsibility, and the Moral Freedom and Responsibility of Business Leaders. *Business and Society Review*, 114:3, Fall, 393–433.

Drucker, P. F., 1973, *Management: Tasks, Responsibilities, Practices*, New York: Harper & Row.

Gifford, J., Green, M., Barends, E., Janssen, B., Capezio, A., Ngo, P., & Nguyen, R., 2019, Research Report April 2019, *Rotten Apples, Bad Barrels, and Sticky Situations: An Evidence Review of Unethical Workplace Behaviour*, London: CIPD.

Harris, K. J., Harvey, P., Harris, R. B., & Cast, M., 2013, An Investigation of Abusive Supervision, Vicarious Abusive Supervision, and Their Joint Impacts. *Journal of Social Psychology*, 153:1, 38–50.

Hibbert, P. & Cunliffe, A., 2015, Responsible Management: Engaging Moral Reflexive Practice through Threshold Concepts. *Journal of Business Ethics*, 127:1, 177–188, https://doi.org/10.1007/s10551-013-1993-7

Johnson, C. E., 2009, *Meeting the Ethical Challenges of Leadership: Casting Light or Shadow*, Thousand Oaks, CA: Sage Publications.

Johnson, C. E., 2018, *Meeting the Ethical Challenges of Leadership: Casting Light or Shadow*, 6th Edition, London: Sage Publications.

Maccoby, M., 2007, *Narcissistic Leaders: Who Succeeds and Who Fails*, Boston, MA: Harvard Business School Press.

Master morpheme list from Vocabulary Through Morphemes: Suffixes, Prefixes, and Roots for Grades 4–12, 2nd Edition, Ebbers, 2010, Available at: www.pburgsd.net/cms/lib04/NJ01001118/Centricity/Domain/174/List-of-English-Morphemes.pdf

Mullins, L. H. & Christy, G., 2013, *Management and Organisational Behaviour*, 11th Edition, Harlow: Pearson Education Ltd. 272.

Northhouse, P. G., 2015, *Leadership Theory and Practice*, 7th Edition, Thousand Oaks, CA: Sage Publications.

Padilla, A., Hogan, R., & Kaiser, R. B., 2007, The Toxic Triangle: Destructive Leaders, Susceptible Followers, and Conducive Environments. *The Leadership Quarterly*, 18, 176–194.

Vocabulry.com. Dictionary, 2018, Available at: www.vocabulary.com/dictionary/irresponsibility

Waldman, D. A. & Balven, R. M., 2015, Responsible Leadership: Theoretical Issues and Research Directions. *Academy of Management Perspectives*, 28:3, 19–29, https://journals.aom.org/doi/10.5465/amp.2014.0016

Waldman, D. A. & Galvin, B. M., 2008, Alternative Perspectives of Responsible Leadership. *Organizational Dynamics*, 37:4, 327–341, https://doi.org/10.1016/j.orgdyn.2008.07.001

Williams, D. F., 2005, *Toxic Leadership in the U.S. Army: USAWC Strategy Research Project*, Available at: www.strategic studiesinstitute.army.mil/pdffiles/ksil3.pdf

Wilson, S. & McCalman, J., 2017, Re-Imagining Ethical Leadership as Leadership for the Greater Good. *European Journal of Management*, 35, 151–154.

Zimbardo, P, 2008, *The Lucifer Effect, How Good People Turn Evil*, Kindle Edition, London: Rider.

6 Creating an IL definitional framework
Content/context analysis

To develop the IL definitional framework, an interdisciplinary approach was taken in order to identify the various terms used to describe the behaviour and practice of those responsible for the corporate scandals; in other words the social construct of IL seemed to overlap (see Chapter 2, Table 2.3; Chapter 2, Figure 2.1).

To verify the degree to which the social constructs within the core fields used to describe the behaviours and practices of managerial leaders responsible for the malpractices were the same or similar, a search for the adjective "irresponsible" was carried out through Google. One source yielded a comprehensive list of 400+ synonyms (see Table 6.2; also see Chapter 5, Table 5.1). The list drew attention to the sameness or similarities in all core fields (see Chapter 2, Table 2.3, and Table 6.1). However, the plethora of terms still needed to be synthesised into a coherent framework that could be used across disciplines so as to teach IL as a threshold concept for understanding RL.

For further verification, having collected and organised the data using CAQDAS, a multi-data analytical process (content and context analysis) was adopted to enable broad and in-depth analysis of the vast amounts of text from the articles obtained. The results from the analysis are now discussed in turn.

Content analysis 1/context analysis 1: "Irresponsibility" – 400+ synonyms list and CAQDAS text search for IL terms identified within text

The first content and context analysis involved using the 400+ synonyms list (Thesaurus.net) to randomly select the socially constructed terms mentioned above; research material scrutinised revealed that these are terms both academics and non-academics are familiar with (see Table 6.2). We decided to take this approach rather than select odd synonyms.[1] Aside from checking

Table 6.1 Constructs of Core Field – Overlapped

Toxic	Unethical	Social Irresponsibility/ Corporate Social Irresponsibility	Dark Triad of Leadership[i]
Harmful	Harmful	Harmful	Harmful
Dishonest	Dishonest	Dishonest	Dishonest
Abusive	Abusive	Abusive	Abusive
Evil	Evil	Evil	Evil
Immoral	Immoral	Immoral	Immoral
Inadequate	Non-social	Narcissist	Psychopath
Selfish	Selfish	Selfish	Selfish
Egotistical	Egotistical	Egotistical	Egotistical
Irrational	Irrational	Irrational	Irrational
Narcissist	Narcissist	Narcissist	Narcissist
Partial	Partial	Partial	Partial
Arrogant	Arrogant	Arrogant	Arrogant
Greedy	Greedy	Greedy	Greedy
Wicked	Wicked	Wicked	Wicked
Incompetent	Incompetent	Incompetent	Incompetent
Ineffective	Non-relational		
Unfair	Unfair	Unfair	Unfair
Maladjusted	Illegal		Unlawful

[i] There are clinical connotations of narcissism and psychopathy, therefore DTL was also viewed from a sub-clinical perspective.

Table 6.2 "Irresponsibility" Thesaurus.Net Sample List

Ambivalent	Capricious	Double-Minded	Erratic	Impulsive
Regardless	Imprudent	Negligent	Unmindful	Controlling
Corrupt	Disregardful	Domineering	Despotic	Extravagant
Extreme	Stupid	Immoral	Impractical	Perverse
Questionable	Self-indulgent	Thoughtless	Tyrannical	Uncaring
Unconcerned	Unreasonable	Untrustworthy	Unthinking	Wrong
Improvident	Uncontrollable	Uncritical	Uninspired	Unwise

for IL synonyms using a technique for coding referred to as "free nodes", all uploaded articles were used for a text search within the themes based on the core IL fields (CSI, SI, TL, DTL, and UL)[2] that had been created from the final mind-map (see Chapter 2, Figure 2.1, and Chapter 2, Table 2.1).

The next stage involved an analytical and coding process consisting of several steps; aside from using samples from the 400+ synonyms list to code the uploaded articles, more specifically, we searched the sentences and whole paragraphs where the terms emerged and these were coded in CAQ-DAS. A large number of synonyms emerged from the text search, and coded sections (sentence or paragraph) were annotated where necessary and linked to memos developed when the initial mind map was created (see Image 6.1) to establish full meanings and, where possible, how they were derived.

The results derived from applying this analytical method drew further attention (although in a more organised and in-depth manner) to the facts that:

A   The terms used in the core fields bear similarity in meaning – understanding, judgements, and reasoning (McInerny, 2005), and

B   That IL can be concluded through numerous observable behaviours demonstrated by managerial leaders (from junior to CEO levels) and revealed through organisational practices.

However, for the purpose of developing further validity (logic) of IL meaning and so on, additional analyses were carried out.

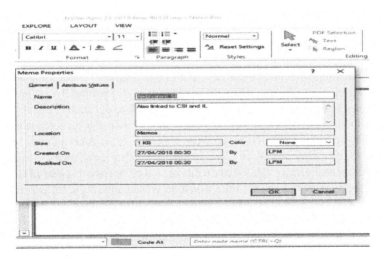

Image 6.1 Screenshot Memo and Annotation Samples Within Broad Fields CSI and IL (x2)

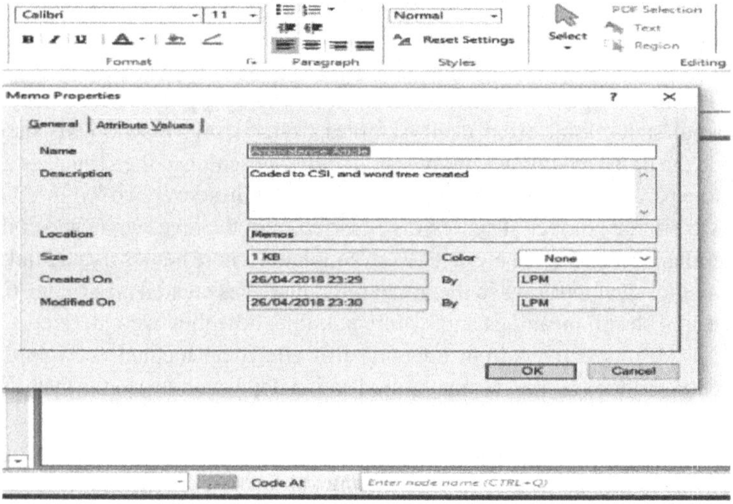

Image 6.1 (Continued)

Content analysis 2/context analysis 2: word frequency test and Word Cloud Samples

The second content/context analysis involved carrying out a Word Frequency Test and developing Word Clouds, which were used to draw attention to the extent to which the synonyms appeared in context, regarded as pertinent mainly because of the accumulative IL synonyms within each core field (see Figures 6.1a to 6.1e). This included taking a closer look at sentences and paragraphs, coding them in CAQDAS to measure the accumulative frequency of synonyms within the core themes, and putting the linguistic element into context. For example, synonyms such as destructive, impulses, corruption, harmful, negative, avoidance, and irresponsible all accumulated within the context of CSI (see Word Cloud Sample 6.1a). A key point to note here is that, while the Word Cloud image shows that terms such as leadership, responsibility, good, social executive, and organisation appeared more frequently (shown by size of the word), in Word Cloud 6.1a, for example, these words were used in negative as well as positive contexts, and therefore were not excluded from the search by using "stop word."[3] Refraining from the use of "stop word" helps to explain a point we make later about teaching IL as a threshold concept of RL. Furthermore, the accumulative synonyms of IL as opposed to the single synonyms demonstrate the high frequency of terms used to depict IL.

Figure 6.1a Word Cloud Sample of CSI Literature

Source: Copyright © Lola-Peach Martins 1 June 2018

Figure 6.1b Word Cloud Sample of DTL Literature

Source: Copyright © Lola-Peach Martins 1 June 2018

Figure 6.1c Word Cloud Sample of SI Literature

Source: Copyright © Lola-Peach Martins 1 June 2018

Figure 6.1d Word Cloud Sample of TL Literature

Source: Copyright © Lola-Peach Martins 1 June 2018

Figure 6.1e Word Cloud Sample of UL Literature

Source: Copyright © Lola-Peach Martins 1 June 2018

Text search, on the other hand, was used to determine how the IL terms/ synonyms identified at stage one of the CAQDAS analytical process were scripted within the articles considered. Similarly, this included taking a closer look at sentences and paragraphs for accuracy, coding them in CAQ-DAS to measure accumulation of synonyms within the core themes, and putting the linguistic element into context. For example, in searching for the term "corrupt" in the context of DTL, synonyms such as "perverted" and "depravation" appeared accumulatively within each article or reference (see quote samples below).

Quote 1

"Crazy Fox" represents a metaphor for a multinational corporation in which an expanded number of managers and employees at various levels of the hierarchy carry out acts of corruption (Luo, 2007). This type of behavioural illness affects both in intensity and depth the plague of anti-CSR. The organisational structure is excessively involved in corrupt practices or it makes alliances with stakeholders in order to get results stronger.

> Source: Luo, Yadong, 2007, "Global Dimensions of
> Corporate Governance", Blackwell Publishing, p. 166

Quote 2

"In addition, every decision is intrinsically value-laden and consequently implies *the question of responsibility*. Responsibility for a leadership decision involves: (1) the realm of competence *of the* leader, (2) *for* making certain decisions and carrying out certain tasks, (3) while remaining accountable *to* a higher authority: his or her own conscience, other human beings, a court of law or God.

What does it mean, for instance, to speak of "profit-responsibility?" . . . The authority to which a leader is accountable may be his or her superior, the capital owner, the public, etc. Profit is therefore what the manager is responsible *for* (that is the second aspect). Profit-responsibility, however, can also mean that profit itself becomes the authority to which the leader is accountable (third aspect). In such a case, the means have been transformed into the ends; profit has been *perverted* and turned into the "Golden Calf. . . . But the issue of responsibility belongs intrinsically to human existence and – in contrast to the situation of animals and machines – human beings distinguish themselves by their capacity for being responsible."

Source: Enderle, Georges, 1987, Some Perspective of
Managerial Ethical Leadership, *Journal of Business Ethics* 6
(1987) 657–663, p. 659

Word Clouds are direct tools, presenting visually appealing text, providing a summarised overview of the most frequent text (Heimerl et al., 2014, Activity Area 18), useful for contextualising IL and working towards a shared in-depth understanding of the concept. Heimerl et al. posited that the method assists processing language *vis-à-vis* sophisticated language and contextualising information.

Activity Area 18 Reflect and critically discuss

Use of Word Cloud

"[Word Cloud] assists with advanced natural language processing, sophisticated interaction techniques, and context information [. . . and is an] approach that can be effectively used to solve text analysis tasks and evaluate it in a qualitative study."

Source: Heimerl, F., Lohmann, S., Lange, M., & Ertl, T., 2014,
Word Cloud Explorer: Text Analytics based on Word Clouds,
Conference Paper, Retrieved 29 May 2018 https://ieeexplore.
ieee.org/stamp/stamp.jsp?tp=&arnumber=6758829,
DOI 10.1109/HICSS.2014.231

Each of the Word Cloud Samples (CSI, DTL, SI, TL, and UL) were based on a word frequency of 1,000 words per core IL field (see Table 2.3, column 3). The size of the texts (for example executive, moral, responsibility, and leadership), which indicated the pertinence of the issues focused on in each of these fields, at first sight shows the central perspectives in the studies. They refer to how executives/leaders behave as well as corporate practices *vis-à-vis* IL (see Figure 6.1a, for example). However, we also ask the reader to consider the accumulative IL texts (such as corruption, harmful, destructive, impulses, bad, irresponsible) which appear smaller in size but put together, because of their sameness and/or similarity in meaning, reveal a high frequency.

The results from the word frequency tests shows that IL leadership behaviours (including executive behaviours as mentioned in the paragraph above) are at the heart of the five core IL fields (see Figures 6.1a–6.1e). The Word Cloud images also provided a snapshot of the key issues to consider when defining IL, and shows similarities between the core fields in this regard. For example, Figures 6.1a–6.1e draw attention to the terms impulsive/impulsivity/impulses and destructive. Therefore, it is possible to use these examples to provide a more meaningful shared understanding of IL drawn from the specific IL fields. Another fundamental point deduced from the word frequency test is that while our study focused on IL, the Word Cloud results revealed that some of the studies we consulted do not focus on IL without making a connection to RL in some shape or form. This is an important factor for academics who are concerned about teaching IL to consider. That is, IL should not be taught without drawing attention to RL or vice versa. A point raised by a modicum of participants at a British Academy of Management professional development workshop in 2015 (BAM PDW) is that concentrating on negativity by focusing on the meaning and perspectives of IL may remove the focus from learning about RL. However, it is clear from these Word Cloud images that teaching IL as a threshold concept for RL (Martins et al., 2015) is not about removing the focus from RL, but rather enhancing understanding.

Notes

1 Such as gutsy, hell-four-leather, sybaritic, vicissitudinous, moonstruck, spasmodic, risible.
2 Corporate Social Irresponsibility, Social Irresponsibility, Toxic Leadership, Dark Triad of Leadership, Unethical Leadership.
3 Computer language referring to how the search engine is programmed to remove a commonly used word. For example "the" or any other word that is not of interest in a search query.

Bibliography

Heimerl, F., Lohmann, S., Lange, M., & Ertl, T., 2014, Word Cloud Explorer: Text Analytics based on Word Clouds. Conference Paper, Available at: https://ieeexplore.ieee.org/stamp/stamp.jsp?tp=&arnumber=6758829, DOI 10.1109/HICSS.2014.231 [Accessed 29 May 2018].

Jacoby, S. M., 2004, *Employing Bureaucracy: Managers, Unions, and the Transformation of Work in the 20th Century*, London: Lawrence Erlbaum Associates.

Lange, D. & Washburn, N. T., 2012, Understanding Attributions of Corporate Social Irresponsibility. *Academy of Management Review*, 37, 300–332.

Luo, Yadong, 2007, "Global Dimensions of Corporate Governance", Malden, MA: Blackwell Publishing, p. 166.

Martins, L.-P., 2009, The Nature of the Changing Role of First-Tier Managers: A Long Cycle Approach. *Journal of Organizational Change Management*, 22:1, 92–123, https://Doi.Org/10.1108/09534810910933924

Martins, L.-P., 2015, HR Leaders Hold the Key to Effective Diversity Management: . . . As More and More Important Decisions Are Taken at Local Level. *Human Resource Management International Digest*, 23:5, 49–53, https://doi.org/10.1108/HRMID-05-2015-0093

McInerny, D. Q., 2005, *Being Logical: A Guide to Good Thinking*, New York: Random House. ix.

Thesaurus.net, Available at: www.thesaurus.net/irresponsible

7 Creating the IL definitional framework

Cluster analysis

Context analysis 3

Cluster analysis is concerned with how sources, nodes, and words are clustered to show similarity and differences between cluster cases for example. Regarding our study, the core fields CSI, SI, UL, DTL, and TL are the main cases and the clusters are also cases within them. The types of similarity are "word similarity", "code similarity", and "attribute value similarity" (NViVo, 2015).

- "Word similarity" example – IL word similarity that appeared in the core fields, and was taken from the 400+ synonym list – see Table 6.2 for word examples
- "Code similarity" example – core fields (sources), which were converted to nodes CSI, SI, UL, DTL, and TL; these were used to code IL words
- "Attribute value similarity" example – the IL word "impulsive" has characteristics (or attributes such as *harm* and *demotivation*), which emerged from texts where it was mentioned. *Harm* is one of such characteristics appearing in more than one of the nodes, and therefore *harm* was one of the values ascribed to the word impulsive, hence forms attribute similarity.

These three similarities can be groups within sources, nodes and texts. For this study, cluster analysis enabled further clarification of the way in/degree to which IL synonyms are referred to, i.e. grouped together in a cluster within the core IL fields – SI, UL, CSI, TL, and DTL (for example see Table 7.1). In addition, the clusters assisted with finalising pertinent IL issues by revealing two main similar cluster cases of IL synonyms: (1) Impulsive/Aggressive and (2) Destructive/Abusive (IADA). We found these clusters useful for developing a definition for IL and working towards a shared understanding

Table 7.1 Cluster Analysis: IADA

Core Fields – CSI, SI, UL, DTL, and TL

Impulsive/Agressive	*Destructive/Abusive*
". . .acting unpredictably and impulsively; and acting aggressively" (Babiak and Hare, 2005).	". . .destructive leader behavior can encompass a wider variety of harmful behavior which is not related to the leadership task" (Schyns and Schilling, 2013).
". . . already outlined, supervisors low in agreeableness and/or high in neuroticism should be more likely to show destructive leadership as they are less concerned about the effects of their behavior and experience greater anger and frustration (and react to it more impulsively)" Tepper (2007; Schyns and Schilling, 2013).	". . . impulsive, irresponsible, and extraordinarily punitive Destructive leadership" Padilla et al., 2007).
". . . sensation seeking, impulsivity, and anger . . . [;] impulsivity . . . callousness, hostility, deceitfulness, and manipulativeness . . . [;] levels of impulsivity and irresponsibility" (Glenn and Selbom, 2015).	". . . bad behavior, self-promotion, abusive and tyrannical supervision, downward hostility toward others, engages in destructive and demotivational behaviors, and narcissistic and authoritative tendencies" (Dobbs, 2014; Schmidt, 2014; Ross et al., 2014).
". . . impetuously aggressive manner for self-aggrandizing" (Padilla et al., 2007).	". . . destructive leadership is positively related to stress and negatively related to well-being. Long-term and frequent exposition to destructive behavior from a person that is in charge is likely to cause stress and lead to lower well-being" (Schyns and Schilling, 2012).
". . . irresponsibility, impulsivity and aggression" (Gudmundsson and Sothey, 2011).	". . . abusive supervision affects an estimated 13.6% of U.S. workers (Tepper, 2007) at a cost of $23.8 billion annually for US-companies (e.g. due to employee absenteeism, employee turnover,
". . . acting unpredictably and impulsively; and acting aggressively" (Mathieu et al., 2013).	"systematic mistreatment/abuse" (Blasé and Blasé, 2002).

of the same. Thus, both clusters were used to develop the definitional framework (IADA; see Figure 7.1).

Figure 7.1 shows the core IL fields linked to cluster analysis (IADA Dendrogram Cluster Analysis; see Figure 7.2). Other clusters further apart from

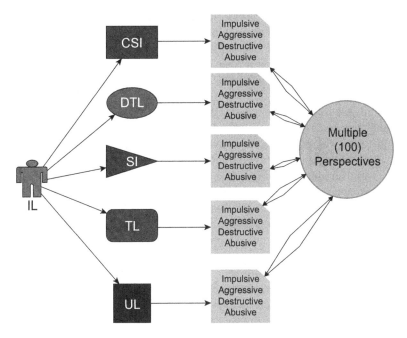

Figure 7.1 IL Definitional Framework: Core IL Fields Linked to Cluster Analysis (Impulsive, Aggressive, Destructive, Abusive – IADA), Linked to 100 IL Multiple Perspectives

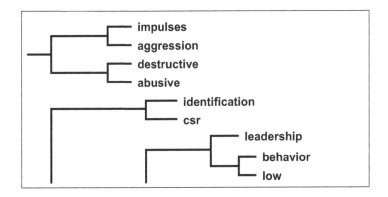

Figure 7.2 IADA Dendrogram Linked to Core IL Fields Cluster Analysis

IADA in the dendrogram also provide a snapshot of different IL cluster cases within the core IL fields (see Appendix 1) worth exploring further and discussing. However, it is not possible to do so here as they deserve greater space and attention than a book of this size provides. What is important to note for now is that all cluster cases or perspectives in the dendrogram, i.e. lower clusters (explained below, also see Appendix 1), are linked to IL as well as RL.

While the word frequency tests (Word Clouds) show the most frequently mentioned words (Figures 6.1a–6.1e, e.g. frequency of words such as leadership, executives, managers, impulsivity, and destructive behaviours), cluster analysis transforms these word frequencies (key words) into paired groups of cases using binary numbers (1 and 0). 1 symbolises where destructive/aggressive appears in the text, and 0 symbolises that it does not appear. Thus, Figure 7.2 represents the total relationship (Clarke, 2018) between IADA and the other clusters *vis-à-vis* the core IL fields combined.

Higher and lower clusters

More than 10 cluster cases emerged, including the higher sets, i.e. the top two cluster cases – impulsive/aggressive and destructive/abusive. The total number of perspectives that make up all clusters is over 100 (Appendix 1). These clusters not only show multi-perspectives of IL, but the different levels of clusters all linked to IADA. Thus, the dendrogram can be used to explore relationships of sorts at all levels, and the links to the higher cluster cases. That is, links from the lower cases (for example base/power, people/ethical, self/sense, evidence/range) to the higher ones (impulsive/aggressive, destructive/abusive). Although lower clusters may not seem relevant at first sight, particularly without access to the full text, from a creative perspective they can be explored further, reflected on, and then used to instigate interesting discussions, hence learning points in terms of generating a more in-depth understanding of IL and RL issues.

To explain further, the clusters represented in the dendrogram (horizontal branching diagram, Figure 7.2) shows similar items clustered together on the same branch and items of less similarity further apart. Items that have a higher degree of similarity based on the occurrence and frequency of words are shown clustered together further up the dendrogram. Aside from acknowledging that the lower clusters are somewhat linked to the higher clusters, the main implications of the results is concerned with the usefulness of the information derived from the higher clusters (impulsive/destructive, aggressive/abusive). These are also portrayed in each of the Word Clouds (see Chapter 8; Figure 7.1; and Activity Area 19 in Chapter 8).

Bibliography

Babiak, P., & Hare, R. D., 2006, Snakes in Suits: When Psychopaths Go to Work, New York, NY: HarperCollins.

Blasé, J., & Blasé, J., 2002, The Dark Side of Leadership: Teacher Perspectives of Principal Mistreatment, *Educational Administration Quarterly*, 38:5, 671–727, https://doi.org/10.1177/0013161X02239643

Clarke, L., 2018, *Using Computer Software for Qualitative Data Analysis, NVivo 11 Training: Basic & Advanced NVivo*, London, UK: Middlesex University.

Glenn, A., & Selbom, M., 2015, Theoretical and Empirical Concerns Regarding the Dark Triad as a Construct, *Journal of Personality Disorders*, 29:3, 360–377, http://aglenn.people.un.edu/upload/1/4/1/8/14182546/glenn_&_sellbom.2015.pdf

Gudmundsson, A., & Southey, G. 2011, Leadership and the Rise of the Corporate Psychopath: What can Business Schools Do About the 'Snakes Inside'? *e-Journal of Social and Behavioural Research in Business*, 2(2), 18–27, https://ejsbrb.org/upload/e-JSBRB_Gudmundssun_Southey_2011_2.pdf

Mathieu, C., Neumann, C. S., Hare, R. D., & Babiak, P., 2014, A Dark Side of Leadership: Corporate Psychopathy and Its Influence on Employee Well-Being and Job Satisfaction. *Personality and Individual Differences*, 59, 83–88, http://doi.org/10.1016/j.paid.2013.11.010

NVivo, 2015, *Qualitative Data Analysis Software*, QSR International Pty Ltd., Version 11, Available at: www.qsrinternational.com/nvivo/home

Padilla, A., Hogan, R., & Kaiser, R. B., 2007, The Toxic Triangle: Destructive Leaders, Susceptible Followers, and Conducive Environments. *The Leadership Quarterly*, 18, 176–194.

Ross, D. B., Matteson, R., and Exposito, J., 2014, *Servant Leadership to Toxic Leadership: Power of Influence Over Power of Control*, Fischler College of Education: Faculty Presentations, 244, https://nsuworks.nova.edu/fse_facpres/244

Schyns, B., & Schilling, J., 2013, How Bad Are The Effects of Bad Leaders? A Meta-Analysis of Destructive Leadership and Its Outcomes. *The Leadership Quarterly*, 24:1, February, 138–158, https://doi.org/10.1016.leaqua.2012.09.001

Tepper, B. J., Moss, S. E., Lockhart, D. E., & Carr, J. C., 2007, Abusive Supervision, Upward Maintenance Communication, and Subordinates' Psychological Distress. *Academy of Management Journal*, 50, 1169–1180.

8 Conclusion of Parts 1 and 2

So far, we have placed a significant amount of emphasis on the increasing problems associated with IL meaning, behaviours, and practices. However, is worth noting that the intention of our study was not a fault-finding exercise – to complain about managers, leaders, or leadership. Neither does defining IL suggest that a leader should be a perfect human being or saint type (Ciulla, 2004); to expect perfection would be unrealistic. Nonetheless, a key purpose of this book is to respond to the call for business schools to do more to improve the RL management curricula, the results of which we hope will have a positive impact on current and future corporate leadership behaviours, hence practices. In the search for IL meaning, 100+ characteristics were unmasked. These characteristics can introduce students to core issues at the heart of IL, and can be useful for reflective practice and encourage debates for enhanced learning in the classroom and beyond.

Maak and Pless (2006) and Burchell et al.'s (2015) studies showed that sustainable organisations and businesses are synonymous with RL. Here we inverted this notion, and addressed the confusion of IL stemming from a lack of synthesis *vis-à-vis* the plethora of terms used in management literature (academic and non-academic), as well as the masking of IL, hence emphasising that irresponsible business practices are a hindrance to sustainability. In other words, IL is strongly associated with social-economic turbulence.

This study found that IL ambiguity, IL, and the lack of a definitional framework for teaching the topic were linked to the shortcomings of business schools – such as inadequately preparing management students to tackle role complexities. We also acknowledged the fact that some scholars might disagree that the need to search for some common ground for IL meaning is important. However, through a critical review of the literature we were able to verify the significance of distinguishing between IL and

RL (for example, the neoliberalist-shareholder notion of the organisation's role or purpose (see Armstrong, 1977, Chapter 1; and stakeholder/shareholder theories, Chapter 2). Neoliberalist-shareholder views together with the plethora of IL terms used have been challenged through our study. Hence, common IL beliefs were established, and enabled the development of a multiple perspective definitional framework. By doing so, we have responded to observations made by Burchell et al. (2015), Kirton (2015), People Management-CIPD (2015), and CIPD/Workday (2016), amongst others. Furthermore, we have responded by observing the IL definition framework gap in RL and leadership and management development studies. Renowned scholars like Lange and Washburn (2012), Hibbert and Cunliffe (2015), and Drucker (1973) implicitly highlighted some key issues linked to the idea of the definitional framework we have created (see Chapters 1, 2, and 5, respectively). While Drucker's work focused more on understanding both responsible and irresponsible behaviours in the way educational institutions prepare students, Hibbert and Cunliffe's work focused on student engagement *vis-à-vis* reflexivity and threshold concepts (also see definition of threshold concept, Chapter 1). Furthermore, Lange and Washburn's study focused on understanding corporate social irresponsibility (CSI) behaviour to comprehend responsible behaviour. However, the increase in corporate scandals, the unexplained bias within the management curricula, and the call for business schools to do more to improve responsible management education suggests that the time is right for introducing radical change in the management curricula. Hence, the idea to develop an IL definitional framework and to teach IL as a threshold concept of RL is timely.

We therefore conclude that refusing to clearly distinguish between IL and RL can be likened to not facing up to the irresponsible (dark side) of leadership or the lack of intellectual integrity generated through (for example) unnecessary bias, particularly where there is no empirically based reason for the absence of explicit IL subjects in the management curricula.

As with many leadership concepts, it is expected that there may be further debates about what IL is and IL ped-andragogy. Nonetheless, if IL is to be taught as a threshold concept of RL, an IL definitional framework consisting of multiple perspectives (real issues that managers and management students can identify with) is necessary (Chapter 7, Figure 7.1).

To develop the IL curriculum, conceptual and operational definitions (Brown, 2000) of IL synonyms have been explored. Hence, from a multi-perspectives viewpoint we were able to develop a definition for teaching IL as a threshold concept of RL (see Activity Area 19, Figure 7.2, and Table 8.1).

Activity Area 19   Reflect and critically discuss

Definition of IL (Impulsive, Aggressive, Destructive, Abusive – IADA)

"Sets of harmful behaviours (impulsive/aggressive and destructive/abusive) elicited by people in leadership positions (including executives), who have been given the authority and power through their position to make core decision which have an impact within and external to their organisation. Such behaviours, if not curtailed have a propensity to lead to unnecessary crises and disasters – negatively influencing others, and causing harm to innocent individuals, organisations, businesses, society, and economies at large."

In the past, academics have been accused of having unrealistic expectations of management students. For example, according to Gosling and Mintzberg (2004, p. 1), "they are supposed to put all [perspectives/subjects] together. . . . They never do." Likewise, expecting management students to make sense of the confusion (RL/IL confusion) without an IL definitional framework seems unrealistic. Therefore, a suite of reflective practice tools, including a multi-perspective definitional framework for teaching IL as a threshold concept of RL, are offered to help students develop a better shared understanding of IL and infuse their learning with practice. Put another way, the framework should go some way in empowering students to gain RL understanding and wisdom.[1] Therefore, the main conclusions for this part of the book are as follows:

1   This study provides an essential response to the call for business schools (particularly the PRME's call) to do more to enhance responsible management education
2   The semantic analysis of the meaning of IL is an essential activity associated with scholarly study
3   The philosophical stance adopted has been effective. It aligns with qualitative meta-analysis, discourse analysis involving language analysis – paraphrasing, inversing, using synonyms and antonyms (Kavcic, 2008). Thus, there are two main contribution of our book here:

  • It provides some clear distinctions between IL and RL, therefore
  • It adds further clarity to the RL education debate, which is a critical step towards management education and curricula development

Table 8.1 100+ IL Characteristics Linked to Cluster Analysis (Impulsive, Aggressive, Destructive, Abusive – IADA)

Irresponsible managers: sanctioned for causing harm	Irresponsible stakeholder	Irresponsible leadership: observable, describable situations	Irresponsible leadership	Irresponsible harm, profitability	Irresponsible actions: quality	Irresponsible actions: Machiavelli	Irresponsible: irresponsibilising
Irresponsible organisations: frequency	Irresponsible companies: legitimised	Irresponsible behaviour: firm/people	Irresponsible behaviour: roles exert power	Irresponsible behaviour: perception	Irresponsible behaviour: conceal or compensate for	Irresponsible: various conceptions	Irresponsible managers: role
Irresponsible firms: in disguise	Irresponsible character: disguised	Irresponsible manner: misguided	Irresponsible: considered if inferior	Irresponsible: naïve	Irresponsible individuals: encouraged	Irresponsible activities: opposed	Irresponsible activities: continue unimpeded
Irresponsible companies: material returns	Irresponsible business	Irresponsible agent	Irresponsible corporations	Irresponsible firms: suffer	Irresponsible companies: techniques	Irresponsible firms: interplay between responsibility	Irresponsible companies: expect to make higher profits
Irresponsible company: seem to have constructive characteristics	Irresponsible activities behind the scenes	Irresponsibility: time and place	Irresponsible means: widely recognised	Irresponsible techniques: opportunities to extract money	Irresponsible practices: increasingly common	Irresponsible practice: advantage	Irresponsible actions: corporate manager, penalties
Irresponsible activities: hidden	Irresponsible: CSR	Irresponsible firm: negative	Irresponsible gains: competition	Irresponsible returns equal on average to responsible…	Irresponsible approach: responsibility pressure to use either or	Irresponsible others	Irresponsible leadership: multiple examples

(Continued)

Table 8.1 Continued

Irresponsible decisions	Irresponsible decisions: risk reduction	Irresponsible decisions: percentage	Irresponsible decisions Government policies	Irresponsible results: poorer countries	Irresponsible practices	Irresponsible strategies People employ	Irresponsible: handling of waste, tax evasion
Irresponsible leadership: hierarchical, extreme	Irresponsible leadership: focus on lessons	Irresponsible leadership: risk of	Irresponsible leadership: notion of	Irresponsible leadership: definition	Irresponsible behaviour: treatments	Irresponsible leadership: crisis of	Irresponsible leaders: take advantage of people; power very high
Irresponsible leadership: endemic	Irresponsible leadership: pervades . . .	Irresponsible leadership: ancestors	Irresponsible leadership: consequences	Irresponsible leadership: indirect consequences	Irresponsible leadership: destructive	Irresponsible leadership: corrupt countries	Irresponsible: corrupt behaviour
	Irresponsible managers: behaviour	Irresponsible: managerial action	Irresponsible: demands, demagoguery, strife, increasing bitterness	Irresponsible: futile	Irresponsible; greed, incompetent managers	Irresponsible: not accept responsibility	Irresponsible: identifying impact
Irresponsible; false trust; not a statesman	Irresponsible behaviour: lacks competence	Irresponsible: vulnerable	Irresponsible: usurpation	Irresponsible: sabotaging national politics, immoral	Irresponsible: national sabotage	Irresponsible: weak, lazy	Irresponsible leadership~; primary cause, strong push for reform
Irresponsible leadership: largely problematic	Irresponsible leadership: most leaders are not	Irresponsible leader behaviour: notable visible instances	Irresponsible leadership: immune	Irresponsible leadership: sector, e.g. health	Irresponsible leader behaviour: stimulating consideration	Irresponsible leadership: actively challenged	Irresponsible leadership: management
Irresponsible management practice: student recognition	Irresponsible: understanding and responsible actions	Irresponsible action: three main aspects	Irresponsible practice: personal role	Irresponsible actions: highlighting	Irresponsible: realisation, struck by past	Irresponsible ways: recognising how people engage	Irresponsible; supplier behaviour

Our study calls for a different approach to delivering RL education (leadership learning and development) and offers a multi-perspective IL framework, which requires management students to adopt mindful/critical reflection on the two main clusters of IL (i.e. IADA) in order to develop shared in-depth understanding.

Notes

1 Wisdom in this regard has been referred to as "the capacity to combine knowledge from different sources and use it Judiciously" Gosling and Mintzberg (2004, p. 1).

Bibliography

Armstrong, J. S., 1977, Social Irresponsibility in Management. *Journal of Business Research*, 5, 185–213.

Brown, D. H., 2000, *Principles of Language Learning and Teaching*, Available at: https://s3.amazonaws.com/academia.edu.documents/40433526/_H._Douglas_Brown__Principles_of_language_learningBookZZ.org.pdf?AWSAccessKeyId=AKIAIWOWYYGZ2Y53UL3A&Expires=1527107963&Signature=40CEy8Ff7yUtJ42AF91YAWbZ9Qc%3D&response-content-disposition=inline%3B%20filename%3DPrinciples_of_language_learning.pdf

Burchell, J., Kennedy, S., & Murray, A., 2015, Responsible Management Education in UK Business Schools: Critically Examining the Role of United Nations Principles for Responsible Management Education as a Driver for Change. *Management Learning*, 46:4, 479–497.

CIPD – Chartered Institute of Personnel and Development, 2016/2017, *Workday HR Outlook*, Available at: www.cipd.co.uk/Images/hr-outlook_2017_tcm18-17697.pdf

Ciulla, J., 2004, Ethics and Leadership Effectiveness. In J. Antonakis, A. T. Cianciolo & R. J. Sternberg (Eds.), *The Nature of Leadership*, Thousand Oaks, CA: Sage Publications. 302–327.

Drucker, P. F., 1973, *Management: Tasks, Responsibilities, Practices*, New York: Harper & Row.

Gosling, J. & Mintzberg, H., 2004, *MIT Sloan Management Review*, Available at: http://web.b.ebscohost.com/bsi/pdfviewer/pdfviewer?vid=1&sid=3c432aef-e10c-4b9b-9b54-5d5883fa3416%40sessionmgr101

Hibbert, P. & Cunliffe, A., 2015, Responsible Management: Engaging Moral Reflexive Practice through Threshold Concepts. *Journal of Business Ethics*, 127:1, 177, 188, https://doi.org/10.1007/s10551-013-1993-7

Kavcic, A., 2008, *Text Linguistics*. Informally published manuscript, English and German Studies, Available at: www.englistika.info/podatki/3_letnik/besediloslovje-I-izpiski.doc [Accessed 10 May 2018].

Kirton, H., 2015, Poor Quality People Management 'Costs Employers £84 Billion a Year.' *People Management, Chartered Institute of Personnel and Development*, Available at: http://www2.cipd.co.uk/pm/peoplemanagement/b/weblog/

archive/2015/09/10/poor-quality-people-management-costs-employers-163-84-billion-a-year.aspx

Lange, D. & Washburn, N. T., 2012, Understanding Attributions of Corporate Social Irresponsibility. *Academy of Management Review*, 37, 300–332.

Maak, T. & Pless, N. M., 2006, Responsible Leadership in a Stakeholder Society: A Relational Perspective. *Journal of Business Ethics*, 66, 99–115.

Timulak, L., 2009, Meta-Analysis of Qualitative Studies: A Tool for Reviewing Qualitative Research Findings in Psychotherapy. *Psychotherapy Research*, 19:45, 591–600. DOI: 10.1080/10503300802477989

Part 3

IL curriculum development contemplation

9 Critical issues *vis-à-vis* developing IL curriculum in turbulent times

Developing new curriculum, content, and educational processes to align with organisational and business sustainability in the 21st century

The quote below by former President of the United States Barack Obama depicts a core aspect of what has been argued in previous chapters, i.e. the importance of understanding "irresponsibility" in order to garnish one's understanding of "responsibility."

A decade after Barack Obama's presidential inauguration speech where he advocated for the need of a new era of responsibility (see Activity Area 20), very little has changed in terms of corporate scandals associated with IL and the lack of education, learning, and development in this regard. Thus, the increase in corporate scandals give a clear indication that economic and social turbulence is still a major global issue, and may be for some time to come. Hence, IL leadership necessitates reflection on critical issues *vis-à-vis* leadership and management development, otherwise known as LMD (Gold et al., 2010), and LMD education. This idea has become even more prominent since the 2008 economic downturn, following scandals relating to malpractices of senior executive leaders in mainstream organisations (see Chapter 1).

Activity Area 20 Reflect and critically discuss

A new era

> "Our economy is badly weakened, as a consequence of greed and irresponsibility on the part of some, but also our collective failure to make hard choices and prepare the nation for a new age. Homes have been lost; jobs shed; businesses shuttered. Our health care is too costly; our schools fail too many; and each day

> brings further evidence that the ways we use energy strengthen our adversaries and threaten our planet. . . . What is required of us now is a new era of responsibility."
>
> Barack Obama (2009), First Presidential Inaugural Address, What is Required: The Price and the Promise of Citizenship, Delivered 20 January 2009

Figure 9.1 provides a conceptual framework comprising summaries of the critical IL issues *vis-à-vis* developing management curricula in the context of teaching IL as a threshold concept of RL. We draw mainly from literature that is philosophically and empirically grounded. For example, literature on ethics argues that the influence a leader has on employees' ethical or unethical behaviour is linked to the managerial leaders' own responsible or irresponsible choice of behaviour (Casserley and Megginson, 2010). Linked to this is the quality of higher education institutions (HEIs), which have a decisive role in the development of leadership competencies in a turbulent economy (Pesonen, 2003). This decisive role includes understanding what learning is essential, how best to design and deliver content, and so on, as these would have an impact on the learner's employability.

In 2007 the Business Industry and Higher Education Collaboration Council (BIHECC, 2007) reported that there were a number of factors contributing to the shortcomings of graduate employability. This was also highlighted through debates on the need for HEIs to do more in assisting students with developing employability competencies. For example, HEIs tend to be blamed for the poor quality of management students and graduates (BCA 2006; Ghoshal, 2005; Hayes et al. 2017; Turner, 2017). Turner's article referring to the Times Higher Education Survey (February 2017), in which the US, Canada, Australia, Europe, and Asia took part, makes it categorically clear that students are graduating without essential and basic skills; also see criticisms of business schools in Chapter 1. Our study showed that there is a general imbalance in the management curricula, i.e. a modicum of attention is paid to IL as a key topic or subject despite a vast amount of studies (including ongoing research) and increasing leadership scandals globally. The curricula bias is particularly noticeable in disciplines such as organisational behaviour, supply chain management, business ethics, leadership, HRM, and CSR and suggests that the curricula is biased and lacks robustness. As indicated in Chapter 1, maintaining a narrow view of an issue (for example) distorts complex issues and overlooks other perspectives (Sadker and Sadker, 2015). This deficiency can be seen in management leadership courses (content) that covertly embed or conceal IL education, and where neoliberal-economist-shareholder views are vigorously promoted by doing

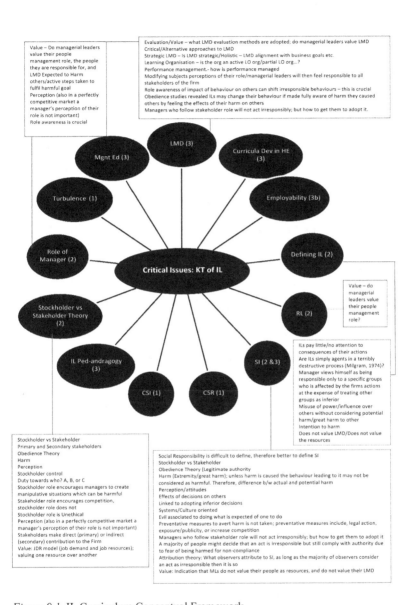

Value – Do managerial leaders value their people management role, the people they are responsible for, and LMD Expected to Harm others/active steps taken to fulfil harmful goal
Perception (also in a perfectly competitive market a manager's perception of their role is not important)
Role awareness is crucial

Evaluation/Value – what LMD evaluation methods are adopted; do managerial leaders value LMD
Critical/Alternative approaches to LMD
Strategic LMD – Is LMD strategic/Holistic – LMD alignment with business goals etc.
Learning Organisation – is the org an active LO org/partial LO org…?
Performance management.- how is performance managed
Modifying subjects perceptions of their role/managerial leaders will then feel responsible to all stakeholders of the firm
Role awareness of impact of behaviour on others can shift irresponsible behaviours – this is crucial
Obedience studies revealed ILs may change their behaviour if made fully aware of harm they caused others by feeling the effects of their harm on others
Managers who follow stakeholder role will not act irresponsibly; but how to get them to adopt it.

Mgnt Ed (3)

LMD (3)

Curricula Dev in HE (3)

Turbulence (1)

Employability (3b)

Role of Manager (2)

Defining IL (2)

Critical Issues: KT of IL

Stockholder vs Stakeholder Theory (2)

RL (2)

Value – do managerial leaders value their people management role?

IL Ped-andragogy (3)

SI (2 &3)

CSI (1)

CSR (1)

ILs pay little/no attention to consequences of their actions
Are ILs simply agents in a terribly destructive process (Milgram, 1974)?
Manager views himself as being responsible only to a specific groups who is affected by the firms actions at the expense of treating other groups as inferior
Misuse of power/influence over others without considering potential harm/great harm to other
Intention to harm
Does not value LMD/Does not value the resources

Stockholder vs Stakeholder
Primary and Secondary stakeholders
Obedience Theory
Harm
Perception
Stockholder control
Duty towards who? A, B, or C
Stockholder role encourages managers to create manipulative situations which can be harmful
Stakeholder role encourages competition, stockholder role does not
Stockholder role is Unethical
Perception (also in a perfectly competitive market a manager's perception of their role is not important)
Stakeholders make direct (primary) or indirect (secondary) contribution to the Firm
Value: JDR model (job demand and job resources); valuing one resource over another

Social Responsibility is difficult to define, therefore better to define SI
Stockholder vs Stakeholder
Obedience Theory (Legitimate authority
Harm (Extremity/great harm); unless harm is caused the behaviour leading to it may not be considered as harmful. Therefore, difference b/w actual and potential harm
Perception/attitudes
Effects of decisions on others
Linked to adopting inferior decisions
Systems/Culture oriented
Evil associated to doing what is expected of one to do
Preventative measures to avert harm is not taken; preventative measures include, legal action, exposure/publicity, or increase competition
Managers who follow stakeholder role will not act irresponsibly; but how to get them to adopt it
A majority of people might decide that an act is irresponsible but still comply with authority due to fear of being harmed for non-compliance
Attribution theory: What observers attribute to SI, as long as the majority of observers consider an act as irresponsible then it is so
Value: Indication that MLs do not value their people as resources, and do not value their LMD

Figure 9.1 IL Curriculum Conceptual Framework

so. In this regard, it becomes clear that HEIs are likely to have played a critical role in the poor quality of some leadership graduates and the lack of employability preparedness (Drucker, 1973, p. 236, also see Chapter 5, Table 5.3). Given the paucity of IL content in management and leadership syllabi and curriculum in general, we can agree with Ghoshal and other scholars' criticisms, and posit that unnecessary curricula bias is highly detrimental to social-economic development and growth.

In view of the well-researched link between IL, social-economic turbulence, and the fundamental role of management schools, HEIs need to consider the critical issues associated with rigid, traditional, and narrowly developed management/leadership curricula. The debate about a well-balanced curricula advances that certain controversial subjects need to be explicitly included. For example, Quatro et al. (2007) suggested spiritual leadership; other scholars have suggested faith based leadership. We agree, but in this book we focus on IL.

Developing adaptive, reflexive/reflective, ped-andragogical approaches to support personal resilience and flexibility during social-economic turbulence and implications for HEIs

To contextualise IL curriculum development, we have considered various scandals associated with social-economic turbulence in the UK and elsewhere (also see Chapter 1 and the endnote below), and theories such as stockholder, stakeholder, and attribution theories.[1] Therefore, we highlight causal and/or casual relationships between IL and social-economic turbulence.

IL linked to the lack of LMD is said to be at the heart of the social-economic turbulence debate (Kirton, 2015; People Management-CIPD, 2015; CIPD/Workday HR Outlook, 2016/17; CIPD/Labour Market, 2018). According to Kirton, developing strong, inspiring leaders is crucial for productivity because poor managerial leadership costs the UK approximately £84bn per annum. A Gallup report in 2013 also revealed that in the US, IL related issues cost the economy over five times more per annum.

In 2016/2017, the CIPD's Outlook Survey showed that approximately 50% of UK professionals believe that senior business leaders lack the necessary competencies required to get the best performance out of their people. Such competencies are often linked to (for example) self-leadership, communication, emotional intelligence, personal resilience and flexibility. Often, this lack of competencies has resulted in IL practices, which in turn leads to increased stress, hence high employee turnover (Azodi et al., 2016; Schyns and Schilling, 2013). Even though various factors have led to the lack of competencies, scholars agree that business schools play a crucial role in developing leaders to address the issues raised by the CIPD and Azodi et al. (2016).

Burchell et al.'s (2015, p. 486) study, though in support of the PRME,[2] uncovered a critical issue about business schools *vis-à-vis* their status in developing responsible leaders through curricula development (see Activity Area 21), which was mirrored by Blowfield and Murray (2011) and Hayes et al. (2017). Referring to responsible management education, they drew attention to the fact that there remains a large gap. Nonetheless, as mentioned in Chapter 1, some business schools have responded positively in various ways. Information on the PRME website indicates over 650 signatories; and other higher education institutions have promoted and developed business ethics and corporate social responsibility courses (or modules).

Activity Area 21 Reflect and critically discuss

HEIs have a long way to go . . .

"Significant way to go before suggesting that responsible management provision is a standard part of UK management schools curricula."

Burchell et al. (2015, p. 486)

Earlier studies, such as Machold and Huse (2010), drew attention to the need for balance, stating that a balanced choice of LMD subjects that are aligned with academic research is required. In contrast, Sigurjonsson et al.'s (2015) study on managers' opinions on how management schools can contribute to providing solid ethics education to students revealed growing evidence on the lack of impact teaching business ethics has on them (Sigurjonsson et al., 2015). The above points relate to curricula issues – what and how a body of knowledge is transmitted in management schools, but in particular, how courses on offer are designed and delivered. For instance, according to Capobianco and Feldman (2006), teachers and students are expected to negotiate what counts as knowledge in the classroom. They ask the following questions: Who determines who can have knowledge? Who determines how knowledge can be generated, challenged, and evaluated? Challenges could be culturally based, i.e. different cultures are likely to hold disparate views on what constitutes irresponsibility (also see Chapter 1, Saadah, 2017). Given the lack of attention paid to IL in the management curricula, negotiations between all stakeholders during development/design stages is an antecedent worth exploring. For example, a leadership development module[3] taught by one of us was revised to include IL within the syllabus, and to develop assessments to meet IL and RL learning outcomes. Former, current, and prospective students participated in the negotiation process by way of offering feedback on the syllabus, assessment, and activities. A pilot study was conducted and further feedback obtained through meetings/discussions and learning journals (also see Chapter 10).

By focusing on curriculum issues, including biases, our book opens an important debate on RL/IL ped-andragogical approaches for classroom engagement.

Notes

1 The UK's financial crises, poor national healthcare and social care, the closing down of large manufacturing plants, increased crime rates (including terrorism), increased natural and manmade disasters, and high unemployment.
2 Principals for Responsible Management Education.
3 Developing Managers and Leaders in Organisations.

Bibliography

Azodi, V., Mohammadipour, M. A., Dehghani, M., Hamedani, A., & Shafiee, H., 2016, Studying the Relationship between Lack of Job Promotion and Career Plateau of Staff: A Case Study in Well Being Office of Kerman. *International Journal of Management, Accounting and Economics*, 3:1, 75–84.

BCA, 2006, Business Council of Australia. In *Changing Paradigms: Rethinking Innovation Policies, Practices, and Programs*, Melbourne: BCA.

BIHECC, 2007, Business Industry and Higher Education Collaboration Council, 2007. In *Graduate Employability Skills*, Canberra: BIHECC.

Blowfield, M. & Murray, A., 2011, *Corporate Responsibility*, 2nd Edition, Oxford: Oxford University Press.

Burchell, J., Kennedy, S., & Murray, A., 2015, Responsible Management Education in UK Business Schools: Critically Examining the Role of United Nations Principles for Responsible Management Education as a Driver for Change. *Management Learning*, 46:4, 479–497.

Capobianco, B. M. & Feldman, A., 2006, Promoting Quality for Teacher Action Research: Lessons Learned from Science Teacher' Action Research. *International Journal for Educational Action Research*, 14:4, 497–512, December.

Casserley, T. & Megginson, D., 2010, A New Paradigm of Leadership Development. *Industrial and Commercial Training*, 42:6, 287–295.

Drucker, P. F., 1973, *Management: Tasks, Responsibilities, Practices*, New York: Harper & Row.

Gallup Report, 2013, *State of the American Workplace*, Gallup: USA, Available at: www.gallup.com/services/178514/state-american-workplace.aspx

Ghoshal, S., 2005, Bad Management Theories Are Destroying Good Management Practices. *Academy of Management Learning & Education*, 4:1, 75–91.

Gold, J., Thorpe, R., & Mumford, A., 2010, *Leadership and Management Development*, 5th Edition, London: Chartered Institute of Personnel and Development.

Hayes, R., Parkes, C., & Murray, A., 2017, Development of Responsible Management Education and Principles of Responsible Management Education. In R. Sunley & J. Leigh (Eds.), *Educating for Responsible Management: Putting Theory into Practice*, London: Routledge.

Kirton, H., 2015, Poor Quality People Management 'Costs Employers £84 Billion a Year. People Management.' *Chartered Institute of Personnel and Development*, Available at: http://www2.cipd.co.uk/pm/peoplemanagement/b/weblog/archive/2015/09/10/poor-quality-people-management-costs-employers-163-84-billion-a-year.aspx

Machold, S. & Huse, M., 2010, Provocation: Business Schools and Economic Crises: The Emperor's New Clothes: Learning from Crisis? *International Journal of Management Concepts and Philosophy*, 4:1, 13–20.

Obama, Barack, 2009, *First Presidential Inaugural Address, What Is Required: The Price and the Promise of Citizenship*, Delivered 20 January 2009, Available at: www.americanrhetoric.com/speeches/barackobama/barackobamainauguraladdress.htm [Accessed December 2018].

Pesonen, H. L., 2003, Challenges of Integrating Environmental Sustainability Issues Into Business School Curriculum: A Case Study from the University of Jyväskylä, Finland. *Journal of Management Education*, 27:2, 158–171.

Quatro, S. A., Waldman, D. A., & Galvin, B. M., 2007, Developing Holistic Leaders: Four Domains for Leadership Development and Practice: The Future of Leadership Development. *Human Resource Management Review*, 17:4, 427–441.

Saadah, K., 2017, The Impact of Samsung Scandal in Corporate Culture in South Korean: Is Corporate Governance Necessary? *Journal Global & Strategies*, 11:2, http://dx.DOI.ORG/10.20473/jgs.11.2.2017.126.134

Sadker, D., & Sadker, M., 2015, Some Practical Ideas for Confronting Bias, Seven Forms of Bias in Instructional Materials, Available at: www.sadker.org/curricularbias.html [Accessed 20 August 2015].

Schyns, B. & Schilling, J., 2013, How Bad Are The Effects of Bad Leaders? A Meta-Analysis of Destructive Leadership and Its Outcomes. *The Leadership Quarterly*, 24:1, February, 138–158.

Sigurjonsson, T. O., Arnardottir, A. A., Vaiman, V., & Rikhardsson, P., 2015, Managers' Views on Ethics Education in Business Schools: An Empirical Study. *Journal of Business Ethics*, 130, 1–13, DOI: 10.1007/s10551-014-2202-z

Turner, C., 2017, Universities Admit Students Who Are 'Almost Illiterate' Lecturers Warn. *The Telegraph*, Available at: http://wwwtelegraph.co.uk/education/2017/02/16/universities-admit-students-almost-iliteratelecturers-warn/

10 Ped-andragogical approaches to LMD in view of applying the IL definitional framework

Leading teams and team leadership

In this chapter we focus on team leaders, leadership, humanistic and social contexts (Gold et al., 2010) and IL behaviours in this regard, as well as relevant ped-andragogies that should be considered in order to apply the IL definitional framework. This is because throughout our 30 years of combined work experience in teaching/working with undergraduate and postgraduate students, we noticed that some student team leaders (project team leaders) working on team assignments display behaviours that are detrimental to team performance, i.e. influencing like-for-like behaviours amongst team members. Our observations have revealed that such behaviours can be linked to a lack of understanding responsibility, and not being mindful of what constitutes irresponsibility. Hence, such students often adopt irresponsible means in dealing with others (peers/team members). When faced with team difficulties leading to team conflict, these pressures cause team leaders to give up hope and behave in similar ways as disgruntled team members instead of adopting soft skills in order to help the team harmonise. In extreme cases, this can result in DTL activities (see Appendixes 1 and 2,). Therefore, we posit that without the development of soft skills required for leading teams responsibly, student team leaders struggle to behave appropriately, and therefore encourage the same behaviours in followers – directly or indirectly (also see Boddy on corporate psychopaths, Chapter 4).

To enable relative change in irresponsible behaviour, which is an aspect of the definition of learning, major tutor/facilitator interventions are required, including additional support from various departments within the academic institution.[1] Our concern is that if disengagement from IL behaviours does not take place while working in teams, and if the issues are not tackled while studying at university, graduates are not likely to be prepared for

Image 10.1 Defining IL in Teams: Student Participation and Engagement
Source: Copyright © Lola-Peach Martins, 2018

employability, but rather are to be expected to transfer the same behaviours to the workplace.

How should the subject 'IL' be taught in the classroom to enhance RL learning?

A change in irresponsible leadership behaviour is necessary for viable organisations in the 21st century and beyond. In other words, responsible leadership is a vital aspect of sustainability (Chapter 1). However, in the words of Terry (2009, p. 55), "LMD is designed around a 3,000-year old pedagogic model called 'teaching'." This is why we propose the idea that IL course designers/developers should consider critical and alternative approaches to LMD in developing IL curriculum. Critical and alternative LMD approaches allow for creativity in terms of developing and designing teaching and learning activities and methods. For example, it is a known fact that game-based learning helps to develop an individual's strategic thinking (Garcia, 2015). The IL Word Cloud Game (see Figure 10.1),[2] which is

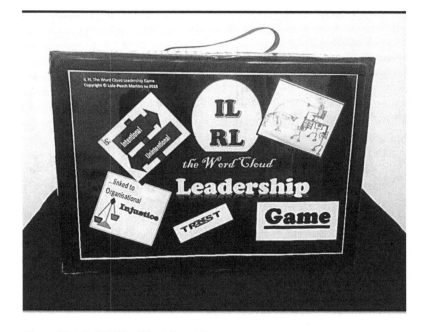

Figure 10.1 IL/RL WordCloud Board Game
Source: Copyright © Lola-Peach Martins, 2018

associated with the IL definitional framework (see p. 61), falls within the category of game-based learning.

Gaming and engagement

Game-based learning encourages reflective and reflexive learning, as well as teamwork, and can increase a learner's flow-state that would otherwise have remained elusive (Pavlas, 2010). Furthermore, it is a known fact that gamification or game-based learning (for example, InerCell and chess) can significantly contribute to transforming potential to improve learning processes (Garcia, 2015), as it increases intensity and interest (Murphy, 2012). More specifically, it helps to develop an individual's higher order skills such as strategic thinking, interpretative analysis, problem solving, and decision-making (Garcia, 2015; Pavlas, 2010; Federation of American Scientists, 2006). Higher order skills such as strategic thinking are key for RL and sustainability, and can increase performance by 50–80% (Murphy, 2012). The IL WordCloud Game is a high intensity game designed to challenge and encourage individual learning as well as teamwork, and is also designed to induce reflective and reflexive learning linked to experiential learning and higher order thinking. While the IL/RL game can be played in an environment not dedicated to learning per se, when used in a workshop setting between teams of students, tutor facilitation may be necessary. Facilitation in this regard involves:

- Giving a brief introduction to the workshop including

    - Ensuring students are aware of the student-centred approach to learning
    - Providing a clear workshop title,[3] as well as clear aims and learning outcomes

- Providing background information about leadership, LMD, and recent news reports (particularly about corporate scandals *vis-à-vis* IL)
- Communicating the essence of learning about IL as a threshold concept of RL
- Communicating the essence of the ILRL game and learning through gaming
- Communicating the essence of learning through failure
- Communicating the essence of recording their learning experience using the interactive reflective learning journal based on the KUWASEP[4] framework (see Figure 10.3 and page 98) immediately after the workshop
- Going through the instructions for the game
- Giving non-participants instructions about taking notes and observing participants whilst they play, and engaging in discussions with their peers about their observations
- Debriefing in preparation for lecture input on defining leadership, leadership debates, and a brief introduction to IL/RL

Image 10.2 shows students learning about IL/RL through gaming/game intensity – their participation and engagement, which is of paramount importance in particular when teaching a sensitive subject/topic such as IL.

Courses and programmes

Gold et al. (2010), Gill (2010), and Edwards et al. (2013) noted the growing popularity of MBA[5] programmes, particularly Executive MBAs (EMBAs), for over 20 years. Other postgraduate management programmes, including management and leadership development courses, are still trending. We searched the internet and found that there is a rise in postgraduate

Image 10.2 Game Intensity – IL and RL Learning in Teams, Student Participation and Enriched Engagement

Source: Copyright © Lola-Peach Martins, 2018

programmes that focus on tailor made leadership learning and development (LLD) and LMD. The CIPD 2018 Management Development Factsheet draws further attention to the pertinence of this subject. In Edwards et al.'s (2013) article titled "Critical and Alternative Approaches to Leadership Learning and Development », LMD studies appear to relate back to the ontology of experiential learning. The crux of their article is concerned with a paradigm shift towards alternatives that:

- Recognise the need for congruence in leadership practices
- Recognise the social context of leadership practices
- Demonstrate an overall appreciation of context
- Show an appreciation of emotions (particularly anxiety and desire in becoming and being a leader)
- Recognise that LLD needs to become inclusive and welcoming
- Show an appreciation of different and innovative LLD approaches, e.g. aesthetic and artistic approaches (non-cognitive methods)

LMD: art-based learning and engagement

Lawrence (2005) also critiqued traditional forms of teaching, and advocated the importance of "artistic forms of expression and their implications for adult learning" (p. 1). He argued that attention needs to be paid to pertinent factors associated with using art to teach adults. Some of these factors include:

* Extending boundaries of knowing by honouring multiple intelligences and indigenous knowledge
* Uncovering hidden knowledge
* Opening up opportunities to explore phenomena holistically, naturally, and creatively
* Deepening understanding of self and the world.

According to Day et al. (2009), adult learners need to understand why the need to learn is critical. It is argued that adult learners tend to be more self-directed, responsible, and internally motivated to learn. From our experience we are aware that if workshops are properly facilitated, experiential learners are able draw from rich sources, make links, and respond to task and problem centered learning. This can be done (for example) through music making,[6] sculpting, painting/drawing, poetry, and short film-making. Research is currently being conducted on the effects of colouring on mindfulness; indications from recent studies show that there is a relationship between both (Mantzios and Giannou, 2018), as well as perseverance and engagement (Eaton and Tiener, 2017). Whilst it can be argued that colouring images does not necessarily involve creating something new, it is regarded as an artistic activity (Lewis, 2016). Art-based teaching can invoke a variety of learning competencies (Activity Area 22).

Activity Area 22 Learning competencies through colouring: mindfulness, perseverance, and engagement

Test how colouring aids your IL and RL mindfulness/reflection – see Appendix 3.

Teaching strategy: a student centered approach to teaching and learning

Teaching and learning strategies such as those that promote critical reflection, reflexive learning (Hibbert and Cunliffe, 2015), mindfulness-learning, and sharing practical experiences encourage LMD students to explore cognitive and non-cognitive managerial influences on [ir]responsible decision making (also see AACSB, 2004). Thus, IL practices and behaviours raise ped-andragogical concerns related to the quality of the IL teaching and learning.

It is important to question:

• What approaches to teaching IL are used to help to engage students and enable them to explore IL behaviours and practices?
• Are the teaching strategies effective?
• Do management/leadership students see the teaching as effective – does it really meet their learning needs?

According to Gold et al. (2010), there needs to be a balance between a human capital (individual focus, planned/formal learning) approach and a social capital approach (distributed leadership, emergent, informal, learning opportunities). Furthermore, IL education curriculum designers and implementers need to be aware of certain fundamentals. They need to be mindful about the apprehension and difficulty that some business management students may have in addressing IL, as it can be a sensitive subject. As mentioned earlier, this is a point strongly raised by some members of the BAM PDW we ran in 2015, and highlighted in our 2017/2018 survey. Therefore, we support the idea that more tutor facilitated/student-centered approaches (over teacher centered ones) that aim to challenge and change the student's conceptual frameworks may be more effective. In this regard, teaching approaches need to focus on what students do, why they think they are doing it, and what they learn by doing it rather than a teacher centered approach to teaching, which is highly instructional, and based on the assumption that such an approach leads to learning (Jackson, 2006).

Student centered approaches facilitated by the tutor, which can be useful for students in terms of understanding how to handle change and conflict, are, for example:

• *"Aim to Fail" Approach*: This idea was offered by a member the BAM PDW IL focus group and is concerned with informal/reflective/reflexive learning, in which students are assigned projects where failure is expected as part of the learning process (in a sense they are given permission to fail), but a reflexive-reflective approach is concerned with moving from failure to success (see Appendix 1 and 2) where students must be reflexive and reflect on their "mistakes" in order to demonstrate knowledge gained/learning. The IL/RL WordCloud Board game (see Figure 10.1) can also be useful in this regard, because first-time

Figure 10.2 Tuckman's S-Curve Model
Source: Copyright © Lola-Peach Martins, 2018

players are likely to score very low marks, which then should encourage them to identify areas of weakness that need to be addressed.

- *"Teamwork Projects and Conflict Management"*: Here students must appropriately adopt and apply teamwork/teambuilding/conflict management models and frameworks. Tuckman's Team Formation/S-Curve (see Figure 10.2) and Belbin's Team Roles (which include company worker, chairman/leader, shaper, ideas person, resource investigator, monitor/evaluator, team-worker, completer/finisher) are examples of such models and frameworks that could be applied. Other scholars have proposed a cyclical version of the model (Bales, 1965). The IL/RL WordCloud Board game can be useful in this regard as well, because teams of two or more people can play against each other, and conflict management skills may be acquired.

  Furthermore, students need opportunities to engage in tutor-facilitated, student-led tutorials in which they can openly discuss IL and its impact using (for example) the IL definitional framework (Chapter 7, Figure 7.1). In these kinds of tutorials sensitive topics such as narcissistic or Toxic Leadership (Schedlitzki and Edwards, 2014) can be carefully explained through tutor-facilitated group/team discussions to help guide the student's reflective process where necessary.

- *'Adopting the KUWASEP Learning Framework'* (see Figure 10.3): There is no doubt that leadership educators play an important role assisting students in gaining soft and critical reflection skills. One way this can be achieved is by introducing students to a variety of practical reflective learning frameworks (otherwise critical reflection frameworks) to assist with deep learning. For example, KUWASEP[7] is a multi-learning domain framework used as a tool for engaging students during their learning process. KUWASEP involves reflections and making short personal journal entries, which can be summarised focusing on key learning points on a weekly basis, after which the journal can be reviewed, assessed, and discussed by the tutor, a subject expert, and/or peer reviewed and discussed. Examples of focused summaries of knowledge written in the journal of final year undergraduate students studying at a University in the UK are provided in Activity Area 23.

"Reflective journals are defined as ' . . . written documents that students create as they think about various concepts, events, or interactions over a period of time for the purposes of gaining insights into self-awareness and learning'" (Thorpe, 2004, p. 328; O'Connell and Dyment, 2011). Some scholars have questioned student authenticity of journals, criticising it as an appropriate assessment method. Others have argued that it can aid student engagement, amongst other major benefits (Baker, 2007). For example, Baker introduced journaling due to students' disengagement from the value of their education, which included activities such as completing, analysing, and integrating the required weekly readings, as well as attendance. In our experience, journals have provided student feedback on their engagement with the assessment as well as with the topic.

When using KUWASEP, students are required to critically reflect using seven learning domains in relation to their learning experiences. The domains are knowledge, understanding, wisdom, attitude, skills, emotions, and self-perceived efficacy. KUWASEP can be used as a mechanism for social change, guiding management students through the process of RL and critical reflections on IL behaviours and practices. That is, bearing in mind that transformation can be negative, a process which Avolio and Bass (1998) referred to as "pseudotransformational."[8] In this regard, KUWASEP can be used with the IL Definitional Framework (Chapter 7, Figure 7.1) and the IL/RL WordCloud Leadership Game (Figure 10.1). For example, used in a combined way, students can develop a balanced understanding of the positive and negative sides of leadership through critical reflection on the words in the Word Clouds. More specifically, students are required to answer questions that relate to IL and RL during the Word Cloud game. After playing the game, it is mandatory for students to use KUWASEP for critical reflections with regards to IL and RL behaviours and practices (all connected to the IL definitional framework and the Word Clouds).

Activity Area 23

Read the following quotes taken from two final year undergraduate management and leadership development students' learning journals, and answer the preceding questions individually. Write down your answers and then discuss in groups of two or more.

Referring to a workshop about abusive managerial leadership *vis-à-vis* LMD, the students stated:

1 "Knowledge: In my opinion [is] one of the most beneficial lessons [in] week 13 whereby we were to create a scenario out of playdoh of our understanding of poor management traits. This has allowed us [my team] to provide our own understanding of the topic."

> MY, Management and Leadership Final Year
> Undergraduate Student

What are poor management traits?

2 "I now understand that irresponsible act of leadership can create more harm than good." (colle, z., 2007, (in Johnson, 2009, p34))

> SM, Management and Leadership Final Year
> Undergraduate Student

Compare the quotes above with what you understand about 'poor management traits. Were you able to make a clear distinction? Was the knowledge different from your understanding? What is the distinction between the knowledge and understanding?

3 "[In] this week's workshop we discussed abusive managerial leadership and explored themes such as unethical and irresponsible practice . . . [teams] discussed what they perceived unethical leadership to be. This resulted in a fruitful discussion between myself and my team members, allowing me to develop a better understanding of the module. The team and I suggested that unethical leadership has the ability to make subordinates more prone to unethical practice. We came to this conclusion based on the individual experiences we have had with unethical leaders."

> ShaM, Management and Leadership Final Year Undergraduate

What do you understand by irresponsible acts of leadership can create more harm than good? Give examples.

4   "I was happy to once again explore the topic of irresponsible leadership. We had already covered the topic in week 3 and it was one of the more interesting topics to cover for me. . . . The team and I built a visual representation of irresponsible leadership through the use of clay modules. Although I was sceptical of this task initially, it significantly improved my understanding of the topic and also served as a reminder to what we had learnt."

Using the materials provided, create your visual representation of IL. Discuss with people in your group.

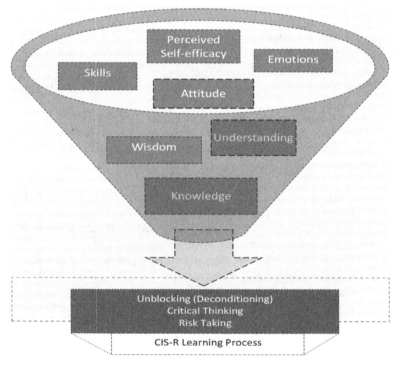

Figure 10.3 KUWASEP Learning Framework

Source: Copyright © Lola-Peach Martins (2009)

Some students may react negatively when studying IL as a result of misunderstanding concepts. Therefore, this is another key issue for curriculum designers and implementers to consider *vis-à-vis* the threshold concept (Burch et al., 2014). In the case here, we treat IL as a precursor to gaining understanding of RL. Knowledge about the theory of threshold concepts should be made clear from the onset, and is in line with the movement of critical management education (CME, also see Dehler, 2009). According to Dehler, CME invokes a social constructivist approach where students actively construct their own knowledge and meanings – engaging in deep learning, pertinent for a globalised world. Furthermore, course designers/developers should be mindful of the differences that students and professors hold of an effective teacher (Hill, 2014). Layne's (2012) study, based on the opinions of 32 faculty members and 233 undergraduate students at a liberal arts college in the US, suggested that students and professors have various views about effective teaching.

Curriculum designers and implementers should also adopt effective teaching strategies. Coe et al. (2014) reviewed research on teacher effectiveness and identified six components that can be used to assess good quality teaching:

1 Pedagogical content, i.e. in-depth knowledge of the subjects being taught; an understanding of the ways students think about the content; an ability to evaluate the thinking behind students' own methods and identify students' common misconceptions. Currently, in-depth RL knowledge is rarely being taught in management schools globally, given the embedding of IL education and a non-defined IL curriculum.
2 High quality of instruction, i.e. "specific practices – reviewing previous learning, providing model responses for students, giving adequate time for practice to embed skills securely; progressively introducing new learning (scaffolding)" (p. 23).
3 Classroom climate, i.e. "constantly demanding more, but still recognising students' self-worth" (p. 3).
4 Classroom management, i.e. ability to make efficient use of lesson time, to coordinate classroom resources and space, and to manage students' behaviour
5 Teacher/facilitator beliefs, i.e. "conceptual models of the nature and role of teaching in the learning process" (p. 3).
6 Professional behaviours (leadership in the classroom and beyond), i.e. reflecting on and developing professional practice, participation in professional development, supporting colleagues, and liaising and communicating with secondary stakeholders.

The six components listed above are based on teacher behaviours that are themselves deemed to be responsible. With regards to pedagogical content and delivering this so that students gain in-depth knowledge of IL/RL, topics can be taught using a variety of methods, materials, and technologies during the workshops. For example, art-based teaching including gaming, animation, model-making/sculpting, music and music-making, poetry, and films – see Table 10.1.

While Layne (2012) and Coe et al.'s studies (2014) put forward notions for teaching excellence, it should be noted here that they do not explicitly draw attention to the need to clarify and emphasise the essence of learning outcomes in the classroom and in course materials (module handbooks, for example). However, this is important for introducing threshold concepts.

Research by Onwuegbuzie et al. (2007), based on 912 undergraduates and graduates at a MidSouthern university in the US, identified nine themes and four meta-themes used to create their CARE-RESPECTED model of effective teaching (see Table 10.2). Interestingly, Onwuegbuzie et al. (2007) found that three of the most prevalent themes endorsed by the college students

Image 10.3 Teaching [Ir]responsible Leadership Education 1: Music and Music-making as a Teaching Method

Source: Copyright © Lola-Peach Martins, 2018

Table 10.1 Video Film Analysis Depicting Two Sides of Leadership – IL and RL, by L.P. Martins (2015, 2016)

Video Film Titles, Genre	Brief Description and Situational Force	(−) Leadership Behaviours and Practices	(+) Leadership Behaviours and Practices
Mutiny on the Bounty: Based on a true story by Charles Nordhoff and James Norman Hall; Screenplay by Charles Lederer	The film is based on the mutiny that took place on a ship called the HMS *Bounty* in 1789. Relations between Captain William Bligh, second-in-command, 1st Lieutenant Fletcher Christian, and the rest of the crew deteriorated. Bligh was an indignant tyrant. The film depicts clear abuse of authority, power, and position. For example, managing slavery; profiteering	Overly focused on the mission; lack of responsible leadership competencies; encouragement of corruption; dishonesty; bullying – verbal, mental, and physical abuse; unjust punishment of crew; unnecessary criticism of crew; deceitful behaviour; abuse of position, authority, power; showing favoritism; determined to make others suffer for his/her failures; lack of emotional intelligence	Determined to fulfil main task through team; objectives clearly communicated to crew
Ghandi: Based on a true story, but dramatised by John Briley	Ghandi's biography as a well-educated man who hoped for and believed in being loving others (showing compassion), truthfulness, fairness, justice, and peace; he believed in holding onto the truth but without being violent – nonviolent resistance. For example, political upheaval	❓	Demonstrated leadership competencies; humane, peaceful human rights campaigner/activist; truthful, loving, and honourable; led by example/servant leadership; knowledgeable; understanding; empathetic; emotional intelligence
Wall Street: American drama by Oliver Stone	Although an American drama, the role of some of the characters in this movie are based on the lives of real people. Gordon Gekko, the main character of the movie, is a very wealthy, unscrupulous tycoon who influences a young stockbroker in such a way that ruins him. The movie ends with Gekko locked up in jail and the young stockbroker learning a huge lesson. For example, Great Depression/economic downturn	Evil desires; greed; encouraged corruption, immorality, ruthlessness; highly unprincipled	❓

(Continued)

Table 10.1 Continued

Video Film Titles, Genre	Brief Description and Situational Force	(−) Leadership Behaviours and Practices	(+) Leadership Behaviours and Practices
Training Day: American crime thriller by **David Ayer**	Alonzo Harris owes a lot of money to some villains. He is a corrupt detective who tries to influence his colleague, officer Jake Hoyt, to become as unscrupulous as him. When Hoyt refuses to indulge Harris and follow in his footsteps, Harris becomes vindictive and plots to murder Hoyt. For example, personal crises: financial	Evil desires; greed; determined to make others suffer for his failures; encouraged corruption, immorality, ruthlessness; highly unprincipled; abused position of authority; psychopathic tendencies; wickedness; selfishness	**?**
The Girl: Fictionalised account by **Gwyneth Hughes**	The film is based on Alfred Hitchcock's *The Birds* starring Tippi Hedren. Hitchcock is completely and utterly infatuated by Tippi. Hitchcock continues to sexually harass her and when she refuses his advances then decides to punish her by plotting and subjecting her to vicious attacks using live birds. He would not relent from torturing her, till he exhausted her physically, emotionally, and mentally; he refused to give her genuine time off work; and manipulates her contract to prevent her from getting work elsewhere. For example, competitive business industry; personal crises	Harassment; bullying; abuse of authority; breach of health and safety at work; tyranny; determination to ruin an employee's career/career prospects; wickedness; selfishness; unscrupulous	**?**
Jesus of Nazareth: Historical drama/biographical	This is a story about the birth, life, crucifixion, and resurrection of Jesus Christ. In the film Jesus preached about faith in God, living a life of love and compassion	**?**	Humane: Authentic/spiritual/servant leader; wise; understanding, knowledgeable about all things, and everyone;

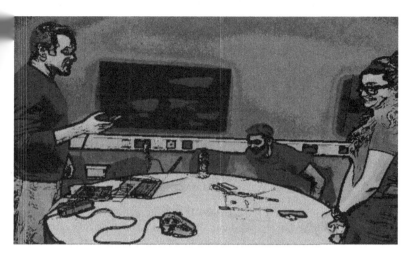

Image 10.4 Teaching [Ir]responsible Leadership Education 2: Music and Music-making as a Teaching Method

Source: Copyright © Lola-Peach Martins, 2018

Table 10.2 Concept of CARE-RESPECTED, based on Onwuegbuzie et al. (2007)

C	Communicator	Service as a reliable resource for students: effectively guides students' acquisition of knowledge, skills, and dispositions; engages students in the curriculum and monitors their progress by providing formative and summative evaluations
A	Advocate	Demonstrates behaviours and dispositions that are deemed exemplary for representing the college teaching profession, promotes active learning, exhibits sensitivity to students
R	Responsible	Seeks to conform to the highest levels of ethical standards associated with the college teaching profession and optimises the learning experiences of students
E	Empowering	Stimulates students to acquire the knowledge, skills, and dispositions associated with an academic discipline or field and stimulates students to attain maximally all instructional goals and objectives

(student centered, expert, and enthusiast themes) were not represented by any of the items in the university's teacher evaluation forms (TEFs). Therefore, this suggested a gap between useful and effective characteristics of tutors and those that students identified as pertinent (Onwuegbuzie et al., 2007, p. 151). This issue supports Capobianco and Feldman's (2006) view that academics are expected to negotiate with students about what counts as knowledge in the classroom.

In view of the sensitivity of IL as a subject and/or core topic, educators need to be cognisant of the CARE-RESPECTED framework, critical and alternative approaches to LMD, and other concepts and theories presented here, in order to be efficient and effective communicators, advocators, and responsible post holders for empowering management students.

Notes

1 This book focues of the IL definitional framework, and therefore does not cover the aspect of additional support in any depth.
2 To purchase the ILRL WordCloud Game, please visit our website, http://team1ljjm.wixsite.com/website.
3 Title "Developing Leaders and Managers in Organisations."
4 Knowledge, Understanding, Wisdom, Attitude, Skills, Emotions, Perceived Self-efficacy.
5 Master of Business Administration.
6 Todd Roache: Life-Coach, Musician, Producer, and Guest Lecturer in Art-based Approaches for Leadership and Management Development.
7 KUWASEP is the acronym for knowledge, understanding, wisdom, attitude, skills, emotions, and perceived self-efficacy.
8 Leaders that learn to become self-consumed, hungry for power and control, exploitative, greedy, and overall immune to ethics.

Bibliography

AACSB, 2004, *Ethics Education in Business Schools*, Tampa, FL, USA: The Association to Advance Collegiate Schools of Business.

Avolio, B. & Bass, B., 1998, You Can Drag a Horse to the Water But You Can't Make It Drink Unless It's Thirsty. *Journal of Leadership Studies*, 5:1, 4–17.

Baker, W. J., 2007, The Use of Journaling in the Development of Student Engagement and Confidence with the Teaching of Music in an Australian Early Childhood and Primary Teacher Education Degree: A New Perspective of an Old Problem. *Australian Journal of Music Education*, 1, 40–49.

Bales, R. F., 1965, *The Equilibrium Problem in Small Groups*. In A. P. Hare, E. F., Borgatta & R. F. Bales (Eds.), *Small Groups: Studies in Social Interaction*, New York: Knopf.

Burch, G., Burch, J., Bradley, T., & Heller, A., 2014, Identifying and Overcoming Threshold Concepts and Conceptions: Introducing a Conception-Focused Curriculum to Course Design. *Journal of Management Education*, 39:4, 476–496.

Capobianco, B. M. & Feldman, A., 2006, Promoting Quality for Teacher Action Research: Lessons Learned from Science Teacher' Action Research. *International Journal for Educational Action Research*, 14:4, December, 497–512.

CIPD – Chartered Institute of Personnel and Development, 2018, *Management Development Factsheet*, Available at: www.cipd.co.uk/search?q=management+development+factsheets

Coe, R., Aloisi, C., Higgins, S., & Major, L. E., 2014, *What Makes Great Teaching? Review of the Underpinning Research*, Available at: www.suttontrust.com/wp-content/uploads/2014/10/What-makes-great-teaching-FINAL-4.11.14.pdf

Day, D. V., Harrison, M. M., & Halpin, S. M., 2009, *An Integrative Approach to Leader Development: Connecting Adult Development, Identity and Expertise*, New York: Psychology Press/Taylor Francis Group.

Dehler, G., 2009, Prospects and Possibilities of Critical Management Education: Critical Beings and a Pedagogy of Critical Action. *Management Learning*, 40:1, 31–49.

Eaton, J. & Tiener, C., 2017, The Effects of Coloring on Anxiety, Mood, and Perseverance. *Journal of the American Art Therapy Association*, 34:1, 42–46, DOI: 10.1080/07421656.2016.1277113, Available at: www.tandfonline.com/doi/full/1 0.1080/07421656.2016.1277113?src=recsys

Edwards, G., Elliott, C., Iszatt-White, M., & Schedlitzki, D., 2013, Critical and Alternative Approaches to Leadership Learning and Development. *Management Learning*, 44:1, 3–10, https://doi.org/10.1177/1350507612473929

Federation of American Scientists, 2006, Harnessing the Power of Video Games for Learning, Track 4, Gamification Ecosystems. *Summit on Educational Games*, 3–43, Available at: http://delivery.acm.org.ezproxy.mdx.ac.uk/10.1145/2810000/2808650/p467-garcia-penalvo.pdf?ip=158.94.254.193&id=2808650&acc=ACTIVE%20SERVICE&key=BF07A2EE685417C5%2E319303F0AC56D129%2E4D4702B0C3E38B35%2E4D4702B0C3E38B35&__acm__=1555167621_c8b36a7220609bc96181816f4fd91f9a [Accessed 12 April 2019].

Freire, P., 1972, *Pedagogy of the Oppressed*, Harmondsworth, UK: Penguin.

Garcia, L., 2015, *Spain's Politicians Reach Rare Education Agreement: Chess Is Good, El Pais, Education*, 12 February 2015, Available at: https://elpais.com/elpais/2015/02/12/inenglish/1423753836_722134.html

Gill, J. & Johnson, P., 2010, *Research Methods for Managers*, London: Sage Publications.

Gold, J., Thorpe, R., & Mumford, A., 2010, Leadership and Management Development, 5th Edition, London: Chartered Institute of Personnel and Development.

Gold, J., Thorpe, R., & Mumford, A., 2016, *Gower Handbook of Leadership and Management Development*, Oxon: Routledge.

Hibbert, P. & Cunliffe, A., 2015, Responsible Management: Engaging Moral Reflexive Practice through Threshold Concepts. *Journal of Business Ethics*, 127:1, 177, 188, https://doi.org/10.1007/s10551-013-1993-7

Hill, L. L., 2014, Graduate Students' Perspectives on Effective Teaching. *Adult Learning*, 25:2, 57–66, Available at: https://pdfs.semanticscholar.org/ae75/d3f6dada0cd6429b4e71477fb07898e1896c.pdf

Jackson, M., 2006, 'Serving Time': The Relationship of Good and Bad Teaching. *Quality Assurance in Education*, 14:4, 385–397, http://dx.doi.org/10.1108/09684880610703965

Lawrence, R. L., 2005, Knowledge Construction as Contested Terrain: Adult Learning through Artistic Expression. *New Directions For Adult And Continuing Education*, 107, Fall, © Wiley Periodicals, Inc.

Layne, L., 2012, Defining Effective Teaching. *Journal on Excellence in College Teaching*, 23:1, 43–68.

Lewis, J. G., 2016, A Neuroscientist Patiently Explains the Allure of the Adult Coloring Book, *The Cut, Creativity*, Available at: www.thecut.com/2016/01/neuroscientist-explains-adult-coloring-books.html

Mantzios, M. & Giannou, K., 2018, When Did Coloring Books Become Mindful? Exploring the Effectiveness of a Novel Method of Mindfulness-Guided Instructions for Coloring Books to Increase Mindfulness and Decrease Anxiety. *Frontiers in Psychology*, 9:56. DOI: 10.3389/fpsyg.2018.00056, Available at: www.frontiersin.org/articles/10.3389/fpsyg.2018.00056/full [Accessed 28 May 2019].

Martins, L.-P., 2009, The Nature of the Changing Role of First-Tier Managers: A Long Cycle Approach. *Journal of Organizational Change Management*, 22:1, 92–123, https://Doi.Org/10.1108/09534810910933924

Martins, L.-P., De Four-Babb, J., Lazzarin, M. D. L., Pawlik, J., & Yakovleva, N., 2015, Teaching Responsible Leadership in the Business Schools: Multi-Dimensional and Pedagogic Discussion. Professional Development Workshop, BAM Conference, Portsmouth, UK, 8–10 September.

Martins, L.P., De Four-Babb, J., Lazzarin, M.D.L., & Pawlik, 2016, [Ir]Responsible Leadership: Addressing Management and Leadership Curricula Biases, IRLCD Report, http://eprints.mdx.ac.uk/19063/1/Report%20Summary%20%5BIr%5Dresponsible%20Leadership...Curricula%20Biases.pdf

Murphy, C., 2012, Why Games Work, and the Science of Learning. Selected Papers Presented at MODSIM World 2011 Conference and Expo. 383–392; NASA/CP-2012-217326, Available at: https://ntrs.nasa.gov/search.jsp?R=20130008648 2019-04-14T08:30:49+00:00Z [Accessed 14 April 2019].

O'Connell, T. S. & Dyment, J. E., 2011, The Case of Reflective Journals: Is the Jury Still Out? *Reflective Practice*, 12:1, 47–59, DOI: 10.1080/14623943.2011.541093, Available at: www.tandfonline.com/action/showCitFormats?doi=10.1080/14623943.2011.541093

Onwuegbuzie, A. J., Witcher, A. E., Collins, K. M., Filer, J. D., Wiedmaier, C. D., & Moore, C. W., 2007, Students' Perceptions of Characteristics of Effective College Teachers: A Validity Study of a Teaching Evaluation form Using a Mixed-Methods Analysis. *American Educational Research Journal*, 44:1, 113–160. DOI: 10.3102/0002831206298169

Pavlas, D., 2010, *A Model of Flow and Play in Game-Based Learning: The Impact of Game Characteristics, Player Traits, and Player States*, Department of Psychology in the College of Sciences at the University of Central Florida Orlando, FL. PhD Thesis.

Schedlitzki, D. & Edwards, G., 2014, *Studying Leadership: Traditional and Critical Approaches*, London: Sage Publications.

Terry, R., 2009, The Great Leadership and Management Development Conspiracy. *Training Journal, TJ*, November, 53–57, Available at: https://dontcompromise.files.wordpress.com/2009/11/thegreatleadershipdevelopmentconspiracy.pdf

Thorpe, K., 2004, Reflective learning journals: from concept to practice. *Reflective Practice*, 5(3), 327–343, https://doi.org/10.1080/1462394042000270655

11 A radical change in the management curricula

It is clear that IL is a major global issue, be it the type demonstrated through the maltreatment of employees in the workplace or external management practices such as injustice in global supply chains. All have a considerable impact on stakeholders, internal and external environments, and societies and economies in ways that are immoral and harmful. This provided an early foundation for our study. In addition to an internet review of management courses and a critical review of academic and non-academic literature in the areas of responsible management and leadership education, SI, CSI, DTL, UL, corporate scandals, as well as the adoption of a pluralistic methodology, we were able to develop a strong argument regarding the need for business schools to be radically innovative in improving management curricula. In particular, we considered why it is necessary to teach IL as a threshold concept of RL for employability and organisational and business sustainability. We drew attention to the fact that the obscurity of IL in various management courses such as business ethics, CSR, and HRM needs to be addressed to enhance RL comprehension (Machold and Huse, 2010). As Laasch and Conaway (2016) put it, sustainable development has become a strategic issue for all organisations, hence "management and executive education have to adapt to this new reality."

There is no doubt that the increasing number of reports on corporate scandals, the surge in the lack of competent leadership, and the impact of neoliberalist views of RL all point to the critical need to radically improve RL education. Even though there have been a number of factors that have contributed to increasing IL practices/behaviours (see for example Ghoshal, 2005; Drucker, 1973), and there are various ways of addressing the IL, there is no doubt that educators (including ourselves) need to be even more innovative and creative in management curricula design and development. It is also clear that the response to the PRME's call, as well as to criticisms about business schools, has been positive. Much of what has been done so far has focused on RL. We have also focused on RL but adopted a rather different approach, i.e. by focusing IL as a threshold concept, with a view to develop IL curriculum to contribute to the solid foundation that renowned scholars have built so far. Hence, we sought to answer two broad questions:

1 As educators, what else should we do to educate future and current managers/leaders *vis-à-vis* enhancing their RL understanding and development in turbulent times?
2 How might one go about developing IL curriculum?

In doing so we problematised the management curricula, explored the plethora IL definitions through various core disciplines, and discovered the masking of the IL concept, behaviour, and practices. It soon became apparent that related definitions were all linked to harmful leader behaviours and practices. The embeddedness and obscurity of IL in management curricula also surfaced as a major issue in that the breadth and depth of IL as a subject or core topic was not being taught in business schools, and thus management students were not sufficiently learning about the significant difference between RL and IL. The idea of teaching IL as a threshold concept necessitated the need to clearly define IL and differentiate between IL and RL learning outcomes. The study and analysis of IL was therefore carried out using CAQDAS.

CAQDAS has been a useful software for exploring existing academic papers, which were carefully selected, and for synthesising the IL literature spread through five core fields. However, further analysis using CAQDAS and other research methodologies needs to be carried out in developing IL definitional frameworks (including ours) and IL curriculum in general. Notwithstanding, what we have provided here is useful for instigating lucrative debates and IL learning, i.e. to enhance RL understanding.

This study has also addressed the issue of RL and IL semantics, and we have argued that it is essential to develop a separate IL curriculum so that management students clearly understand the differences, steering as far as possible from presenting IL in an oxymoronic way. It is clear from our studies that IL is associated with evil and harmful behaviour (intentional and unintentional). Furthermore, given the propensity of the depth of knowledge that can be gained through our findings (development of Word Clouds, IL definitional framework, and IL definition – see Chapters 6, 7, and 8), we conclude that treating IL as a threshold concept could enhance the student's knowledge and understanding of RL and challenge IL behaviours (Hibbert and Cunliffe, 2015; Burch et al., 2014; Lange and Washburn, 2012, also see Chapter 1). Therefore, it is imperative to introduce IL as a compulsory topic in the leadership syllabus and a subject in the management curricula at undergraduate and postgraduate levels.

Working toward differentiating between IL and RL should facilitate the learner's development of soft skills and behaviours, such as the emotional intelligence (Thomas, 2015) pertinent for RL. Thomas raised the question: "[What can be done in order for Management Schools, or indeed management education, to remain relevant and viable]?" and in response suggested that it was extremely important to develop the student's emotional intelligence skills. Such skills include expertise in being critical of one's behaviour and expertise in synthesising knowledge. A constructive critique, whether of self, others, or a concept, enables students to understand a broader set of perspectives about problems, and synthesis on the other hand helps to integrate thinking between IL and RL, for example. One way in which this could be done is by reflecting on the Word Clouds (see Figures 6.1a–6.1e) which were used to create the ILRL Word Cloud Leadership Game (see Figure 10.1).

We paid attention to ped-andragogical matters and discussed issues around approaches and methods required to engage students in IL learning, as well as engagement in developing RL competencies (see Chapter 10). Such approaches include those which acknowledge that managerial leaders are faced with major challenges, learn in different ways, and have preferred learning styles (Gold et al., 2010). From the 1960s onwards, it was observed that adults learned differently (andragogy) and therefore must be considered differently when educating them in comparison to the way children are taught (pedagogy) (Knowles et al., 2005). We conclude that both are pertinent to IL and RL education in that we see pedagogy and andragogy as an integrated learning concept – ped-andragogy that supports continuous professional development (CPD) and life-long learning.

It is worth noting that the debate about the direct impact of LMD on organisational and business performance still exists. In other words, there are many assumptions made about the outcome of investing in LMD because not all managers consciously seek to learn, while others are prevented from putting what they have learnt into practice as a result of organisational barriers that inhibit their intentions (Gold et al., 2010; Martins, 2008). Notwithstanding, it is clear that a change in behaviour occurs as a result of learning (Gold et al., 2016). Hence we conclude that while there are many assumptions made about the benefits of LMD and education, IL education is imperative for RL understanding and development. Therefore, we posit that it is important to consider a whole range of factors influencing managerial leadership performance/RL practices and behaviours[1] when developing IL curriculum (see Activity Area 24).

Activity Area 24 Reflect and critically discuss

**Factors influencing managerial leadership
(four factor framework)**

Martins (2007) identified four key factors influencing managerial leader's performance:

- Clarity of their people management role (R)
- Perceptions and attitudes towards their role (P/A)
- Training/development (T/D)
- Broader organisational support (BOS)

Gold et al. (2010) identified five factors that hinder the managerial leaders learning, hence performance:

- Lack of recognition that a learning need exists (P/A)
- Lack of assessment of the relevant needs (BOS)
- A lack of understanding on the part of the organisation that learning must be given high priority in order to be effective (BOS, P/A, T/D)
- The presence of defensive routines which actively prevent learning (R, P/A, BoS, T/D)
- Failure of managers to give stimulus, encouragement, and help (R, P/A, BoS, T/D)

Activity Area 25 Reflect and critically discuss

Description of reflexivity

"Reflexivity works at two levels – being self-reflexive about our own beliefs, values, and so on, and the nature of our relationships with others, what we say, and how we treat them (Cunliffe, 2016); and being critically reflexive about organisational practices, policies, social structures, and knowledge bases. both self- and critical reflexivity are important in working toward ethical, responsive, and responsible organisations."

Cunliffe, A.I., 2016, On becoming a Critically Reflexive
Practitioner . . . *Journal of Management Education,*
doi:10.1177/1052562916668919, P741

Closing statement: a radical change in the management curricula

This book has presented a case for a radical change in the management curricula, globally. Hence, business (management) schools that wish to engage management students in developing RL understanding should consider the potential benefits of introducing IL as a threshold concept for gaining a shared, in-depth understanding of RL.

To develop IL curriculum, barriers need to be identified. These may include:

a   Ignoring ideas from subject experts: Instead of ignoring ideas from subject experts, top-down support from Deans, Heads of Departments, Directors of Courses, and Course Leaders, is essential.
b   Ignoring bottom-up involvement: Student buy-in in the form of feedback on course development and design using various methods for this purpose is essential.
c   Management curricula bias:[2] Refusing to pay attention to IL as an equally important subject as RL, and by simply treating it as an "elephant in the room" (the fact or truth no one wants to talk about), thus hiding it deep within positively labelled subjects and topics, has to come to an end. This can be done by treating IL as a threshold concept for teaching RL: making it a subject and core topic in its own right, and designing assessments with clearly defined IL and RL learning outcomes; and emphasising the criticality of IL education to improve and develop a shared understanding of RL *vis-à-vis* professional practices in work organisations, particularly during social, economic, and political turbulence.
d   Cultural issues: The organisational culture may prevent curriculum development if the organisation is resistant to change, toxic, or adverse to risk-taking.

Significance of the book

Regarding the significance of this book, it has explored IL terminology, made clear the implications for IL ped-andragogy, drew attention to relationships between curricula bias and work organisation IL practices and behaviours, introduced a definitional framework for understanding IL curricula development, and provided a synthesised IL definition.

Future research

This book opens pathways for future research; however we do not doubt that by addressing IL directly through more robust and well-designed curricula, further RL understanding and development is likely. Therefore, future research should consider cross-cultural, comparative, global studies, and adopt various methodologies, particularly ones that are innovative.

Work in the area of IL curriculum development is still in the early stages, and the importance of more research that addresses management curricula

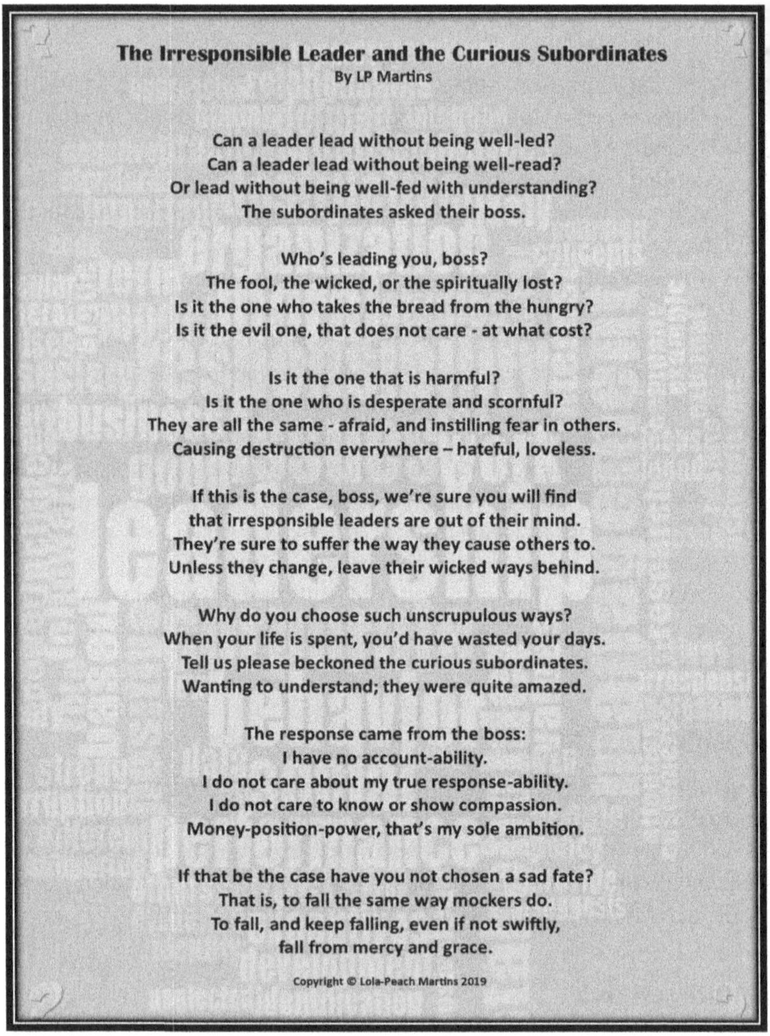

The Irresponsible Leader and the Curious Subordinates
By LP Martins

Can a leader lead without being well-led?
Can a leader lead without being well-read?
Or lead without being well-fed with understanding?
The subordinates asked their boss.

Who's leading you, boss?
The fool, the wicked, or the spiritually lost?
Is it the one who takes the bread from the hungry?
Is it the evil one, that does not care - at what cost?

Is it the one that is harmful?
Is it the one who is desperate and scornful?
They are all the same - afraid, and instilling fear in others.
Causing destruction everywhere – hateful, loveless.

If this is the case, boss, we're sure you will find
that irresponsible leaders are out of their mind.
They're sure to suffer the way they cause others to.
Unless they change, leave their wicked ways behind.

Why do you choose such unscrupulous ways?
When your life is spent, you'd have wasted your days.
Tell us please beckoned the curious subordinates.
Wanting to understand; they were quite amazed.

The response came from the boss:
I have no account-ability.
I do not care about my true response-ability.
I do not care to know or show compassion.
Money-position-power, that's my sole ambition.

If that be the case have you not chosen a sad fate?
That is, to fall the same way mockers do.
To fall, and keep falling, even if not swiftly,
fall from mercy and grace.

Copyright © Lola-Peach Martins 2019

Image 11.1 The Irresponsible Leader and the Subordinates

imbalance should not be underestimated. Therefore we conclude that, if RL education, learning, and development is deemed instrumental in positively influencing professional practice – a message strongly advocated by the PRME suggests (Sroufe et al., 2015) – then IL research, education, learning, and development is equally vital.

As with all academic studies, there are limitations. The main limitations here are the lack of quantitative evidence into student learning outcomes *vis-à-vis* the application of the multi-perspectives IL framework; our research in this regard is already in progress. Notwithstanding, it is hoped that readers will:

- Engage with this book
- Find it useful
- Use it to demonstrate the importance of understanding the difference between teaching IL knowledge, and the knowledge required to teach IL (Ball et al., 2008), as well as
- Use it to instigate further debate.

Notes

1 Factors influencing leadership performance/RL practices and behaviours also draw attention to work-based learning (WBL) and practice-based learning (PBL) activities, where the former focuses on actions/tasks forming the manager's practice, while simultaneously allowing for reflexivity (see Activity Area 25) and reflection. Hence, WBL is typically about a change in thinking and behaviour, and PBL is typically about specific action or practice (Gold et al., 2010). Both are worth considering for ensuring a variety of ped-andragogies are considered.
2 There are a number of management curricula biases. Here we refer to bias in terms of the absence of IL as a topic and subject in its own right.

Bibliography

Ball, D. L., Thames, M. H., & Phelps, G., 2008, Content Knowledge for Teaching What Makes It Special? *Journal of Teacher Education*, 59:5, 389–407.

Burch, G., Burch, J., Bradley, T., & Heller, A., 2014, Identifying and Overcoming Threshold Concepts and Conceptions: Introducing a Conception-Focused Curriculum to Course Design. *Journal of Management Education*, 39:4, 476–496.

Cunliffe, A. L., 2016, *On Becoming a Critically Reflexive Practitioner* Redux: What Does It Mean to Be Reflexive? *Journal of Management Education*, 40:6, 740–746.

Drucker, P. F., 1973, *Management: Tasks, Responsibilities, Practices*, New York: Harper & Row.

Ghoshal, S., 2005, Bad Management Theories Are Destroying Good Management Practices. *Academy of Management Learning & Education*, 4:1, 75–91.

Gold, J., Thorpe, R., & Mumford, A., 2010, *Leadership and Management Development*, 5th Edition, London: Chartered Institute of Personnel and Development.

Gold, J., Thorpe, R., & Mumford, A., 2016, *Gower Handbook of Leadership and Management Development*, Oxon: Routledge.

Hibbert, P. & Cunliffe, A., 2015, Responsible Management: Engaging Moral Reflexive Practice through Threshold Concepts. *Journal of Business Ethics*, 127:1, 177, 188, https://doi.org/10.1007/s10551-013-1993-7

Knowles, M. S., Holton, E. F., & Swanson, R. A., 2005, *The Adult Learner: The Definitive Classic in Adult Education and Human Resource Development*, 6th Edition, Burlington, MA: Elsevier.

Laasch, O. & Conaway, R. N., 2016, *Responsible Business: The Textbook for Management Learning, Competence and Innovation*, 2nd Edition, Sheffield: Greenleaf.

Lange, D. & Washburn, N. T., 2012, Understanding Attributions of Corporate Social Irresponsibility. *Academy of Management Review*, 37, 300–332.

Machold, S. & Huse, M., 2010, Provocation: Business Schools and Economic Crises: The Emperor's New Clothes: Learning from Crisis? *International Journal of Management Concepts and Philosophy*, 4:1, 13–20.

Martins, L.-P., 2007, A Holistic Framework for the Strategic Management of First Tire Managers. *Management Decision*, 45:3, 616–641.

Martins, L.-P., 2008, *The Strategic Management of First-Tier-Managers: A British Aerospace Engineering Manufacturing Company Case Study*. London: Middlesex University. PhD thesis uk.bl.ethos.548923.

Sroufe, R., Sivasubramaniam, N., Ramos, D., & Saiia, D., 2015, Aligning the PRME: How Study Abroad Nurtures Responsible Leadership. *Journal of Management Education*, 39:2, 244–275.

Thomas, H., 2015, *The Business Education Jam, Research Focus Business and Management*, First Issue, Boston University Questrom School of Business. 9–11, Available at: www.emeraldgrouppublishing.com/bizfocus/pdf/bizfocus_mag.pdf [Accessed 27 December 2015].

Appendices

Appendix 1

Full dendrogram: Core IL fields cluster analysis

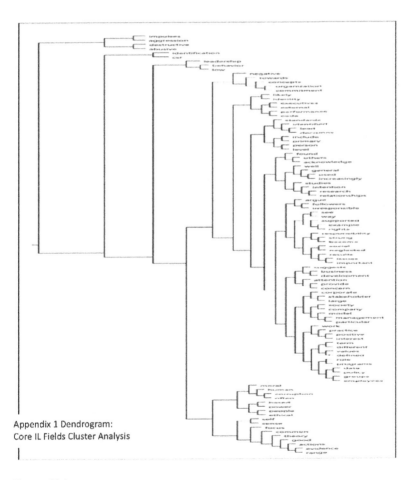

Appendix 1 Dendrogram:
Core IL Fields Cluster Analysis

Figure A1.1

Appendix 2
DTL case study

Case Description (I) Coaching a Team of Management Consulting Students *Vis-à-vis* Their Dark Triad (Dt) of Leadership: A Case Study Ex Post Facto

The consulting team members are referred to as MC1, MC2, MC3, MC4

Management Consulting Team Name: CBiBs

Team description by the team

"[We are a team of] four international, proactive, positive Music Business and Arts Management students. As part of our BA programme we are undertaking a course in management consulting. The team name [reflects] how we approach our work as a team, and our team believes that the logo [shows] our creative ideas and skills. Much like bees, hard work, efficiency, and teamwork are our main defining traits. All four members always dive into the task at hand and pull all efforts together to solve problems in the most efficient and practical way. With strong team diversity – all members [stemming from] different backgrounds, and having [various] experiences, and hobbies, we are constantly expanding the sphere of knowledge and try to apply it in practice in the most effective way. Creative and open minded, we are ready to face and explore any challenges that come our way in order to achieve the set goals."

Self-description of CBiBs' team members

Using the framework for Belbin's team roles (Belbin, 1993) as a guide, each member described their role.

> *MC1:* Female from North Europe; *Team leader*; work experience involved working in various environments, with others/multicultural

teams, and in a leadership capacity. Has also worked with horses (stable manager), is hardworking and patient; has learnt to be diplomatic, observe situations from different perspectives. Is punctual, honest, dependable, is able to give constructive criticism; seeks to continuously develop self and others.

MC2: Female from Southeast Europe; *Company worker, resource investigator, completer/finisher, and team-worker*; she described herself as an enthusiastic extrovert, and very communicative. Work experience – professional musician (sings and plays piano) and worked in advertising for three years. Has achieved supervisory/managerial positions; creative and business oriented person, open to ideas of others leading to team satisfaction. Passionate about music; self-motivated and proactive; understands diversity of human characters (strongest competencies in this regard); perfectionist, and keeps busy by exploring new opportunities, ideas in order to turn them into practical actions.

MC3: Male from West Africa; *Shaper, ideas person, and team-worker*; business owner – production company; he says that he has learnt to be creative and introduce new ideas; makes effort to develop personal business skills; is well-travelled/lived in various countries which has formed his understanding of different cultures; is an enthusiastic learner and enjoys expanding his knowledge within the music business arena; he says his energetic and his positive personality allows him to work well with others while displaying hard work ethic and a professional demeanour.

MC4: Female from Far East Asia; *shared leadership role, ideas person, completer/finisher, and very strong team-worker*; she says that she has successfully built her career in cultural event promotions in the UK and Japan; has been involved in many different projects from music gigs to fashion shows; she describes herself as outgoing, creative, reliable, diligent, and flexible (strongest traits; able to build strong, long-lasting relationships (for example, clients)); makes an effort to introduce new/creative ideas to enhance teamwork, and to make the experience of an event richer; has often taken up the role of financial manager to gain greater understanding of personal responsibility and to bolster the quality of her work, making her mindful of time and management deadlines; says she is always on the lookout to improve her skills, and significantly benefit events she manages/organises to create a unique and unforgettable experience.

DT behaviours of CBiBs observed by the module leader/ tutor (MLT) during the management consulting project

During the consulting project, which CBiBs carried out for a well-known UK music producer/publisher, the DT behaviours they exhibited contradicted their self-descriptions and their team profile (also see *Self-Description of CBiBs' Team Members*) for approximately 17 weeks.

Between learning weeks 4 to 21 there were constant attempts to betray each other. Manipulation ensued with crude attempts to outsmart each other as well as the MLT. Poor time management was a frequent occurrence. There was a constant display of false grandiosity/superiority – a deliberate overestimation of self-power, which led to the self-creation of destructive barriers the students placed along their own individual learning paths and that of their other team members. They intentionally deceived each, claiming to have abilities, skills, and competencies they did not possess. Attempts were made to do the same to their MLT to ensure that they succeeded in getting their own way. This was evidenced during face-to-face meetings with the MLT and documents submitted to him. These documents included the team résumé, team contract, and peer assessments, and showed substantial overrating of self and peers, ignoring what they had been taught during teamwork and team building workshops. Furthermore, CBiBs bragged about how well they had performed on other modules to the MLT and each other. When inquiries were made about their contribution to the team conflict/turmoil and work carried out for the project, it was revealed that false claims were made with regards to completing tasks. When asked to provide the work, CBiBs could not. They reported acts of discrimination towards each other (accusation between team members about racism and genderism) in attempts to convince the MLT to remove disliked people from the team. In this regard there was some evidence of disconnectedness from the essence of team diversity and respect towards each other. Continuous attempts were made to destroy and jeopardise each other's prospects of passing the course. To this end, they hoped that they would be given an alternative assessment. This was confirmed during meetings held with the MLT when MC1 and MC4 requested alternative assessments, and further investigations carried out by the MLT revealed that they had deliberately exaggerated their claims against a particular member of their team.

Each member of the team played their part in absenteeism from team meetings and failure to participate in teamwork activities. Failure to take responsibility for their destructive actions grew, and therefore turmoil between team members increased. They were highly insensitive towards each other's learning needs, therefore void of their own weaknesses even when highlighted by each other during the facilitated workshops. There were threats of violence by MC3 towards his team members. He discriminated against their age by constantly telling them that they were "kids" and that he did "not [regard them as] age mates." This was a term he used when reporting his team members to the MLT. During the team disputes MC2 remained aloof and disengaged. MC2's attendance record was particularly bad; whenever the MLT asked how the team was doing/performing, she would state that everything was going well, but never produced any evidence to this effect.

MC1 and MC4 tended to display negative emotions during one-to-one meetings with the MLT. Both were initially very tearful and angry when reporting on other team members. However, it soon became clear that this was a manipulative tactic each used in order to be convincing. Sometimes their anger was directed towards the MLT, particularly when this tactic failed to achieve the objective, and when he probed for:

- Details and/or evidence (such as emails they claimed to send to other members of their team regarding the incidents being reported),
- Whether they had made any attempts to consider and use the tools available to manage critical incidents (for example see **Managing** Disruptive Behaviours/Situations, Appendix 3), and
- Whether they had made any attempts to apply the theories and concepts they had been taught.

The MLT addressed the subject of the psychological contract, which he initially drew attention to during the first workshop as he felt that it was important to clarify student's expectations and concerns, as well as his. In their initial responses they made clear that there were no concerns about working in a team and the module. A modicum of expectations was highlighted, but this was mainly about gaining knowledge about the role of the consultant. Another expectation was about getting a very high grade. Regarding their concerns, they chose to be pretentious.

The MLT was initially surprised by the irresponsible behaviours demonstrated by CBiBs because despite teaching them about cultural difference and distinguishing between ability, skills, and competencies to assist with writing their team résumé, CBiBs still made false claims in preparation for their interviews with the MLT. Each member had been given information about the purpose of the interviews, which was to assist with the Client/ Organisation selection process. Furthermore, despite the fact that the MLT had explained that the purpose of his tutor/facilitator role, i.e. to offer constructive criticisms and ask questions that challenged their thinking, as well as his duty of care and compassion, CBiBs treated him disrespectfully.

Theories and concepts taught were ignored, and the students behaved as if they "knew it all." This haughty attitude preceded the team conflict/turmoil, and continued up to week 21, albeit reductions in their DT behaviours were gradual – faster in MC1 than MC2, MC3, and MC4. Overall, none of them acknowledged their own irresponsible behaviours/attitudes, which seemed at the time to be seared. They removed the focus from self, and instead focused on other members of the team and the MLT. On the plus side, the CBiBs had a good amount of field knowledge about the creative industry, marketing, and some aspects of events management by the time they started their research, and were also aware of the various types of consultant roles and consulting interventions. However, in terms of understanding RL and personal effectiveness (for example self-leadership, teamwork, personal effectiveness – time management, organising and planning, effective communication including active listening/discussing/dialoguing, negotiating, managing meetings, and decision making), they lacked in competencies, and initially refused to accept that there were any DT behavioural issues. Overall, the DT behaviours included:

- Bullying their peers; attempting to bully the MLT
- Sending inappropriate WhatsApp messages to peers
- Sending mediocre emails to their clients and expecting the client to respond/be at their beck-and-call
- Disagreeing with the need to understand cultural difference/socialisation
- Not caring about attending team meetings and workshops
- Not caring about being self-reflective
- Having a hostile attitude towards learning
- Forcing their views on the MLT and each other
- Giving different versions of incidents to the programme leader and MLT, hence, being manipulative if they felt that the MLT had not sided with them during meetings they arranged to have with her
- Being vindictive when they failed to get their way, for example bullying tactics
- Being vindictive if the MLT did not afford them extra time to complete a task, that is after she discovered that there was no justifiable reason for the late submission of post workshop tasks
- Displaying a sense of entitlement towards the MLT and each other
- Showing lack of emotion (lack of empathy towards others)

While the DT behaviours/attitudes of the students lasted for 17 out of 24 learning weeks, educative coaching played a critical role in CBiB's responsible leadership learning and development. Consequently, the team was able to overcome individual learning barriers and successfully complete their assessments. Their coursework grades varied – pass, merit, and a distinction.

Summary of the literature *vis-à-vis* the DT

The study of dark personality has been well documented, even from a historical perspective (see for example Harms and Spain, 2015). Albeit concerning the coaching of project management teams, *vis-à-vis* DT, the same cannot be said.

In view of the work of Jones and Figueredo (2013), Matheieu et al. (2014), Schyns and Schilling (2013), and Paulhus and Williams (2002), it can be presumed that the behaviours exhibited by the management consulting team fall within the overlapping categories of the dark triad of leadership – narcissism, Machiavellianism, and sub-clinical psychopathy. Likewise, these behaviours are categorised into what Matheieu et al. (2014) referred to as the common behaviours *vis-à-vis* the dark side of leadership – toxic, abusive, tyrannical, and destructive.[1] Even though the behaviour/attitudes lived out by the students for a lengthy duration can be deemed as their dark triad of leadership, and the students struggled with the process of acculturation, through educative coaching they were eventually able to overcome some of their learning barriers, hence enhance their performance.

Note

1 Also see in Matheieu et al. (2014), Lipman-Blumen (2008), Tepper (2000), Ashforth (1994), and Einarsen et al. (2007).

Bibliography

Ashforth, B., 1994, Petty Tyranny in Organizations. *Human Relations*, 47, 755–77.

Babiak, P., & Hare, R. D., 2006, *Snakes in Suits: When Psychopaths Go to Work*, New York, NY: HarperCollins.

Belbin, R. M., 1993, *Team Roles at Work*, Oxford: Butterworth-Heinemann.

Einarsen, S., Aasland, M. S., & Skogstad, A., 2007, Destructive Leadership Behaviour: A Definition and Conceptual Model. *Leadership Quarterly*, 18, 207–216, http://dx.doi.org/10.1016/j.leaqua.2007.03.002

Harms, P. D. & Spain, S. M., 2015, Beyond the Bright Side: Dark Personality at Work. *Applied Psychology*, 64:1, 15–24.

Jones, D. N. & Figueredo, A. J., 2013, The Core of Darkness: Uncovering the Heart of the Triad. *European Journal of Personality*, 27, 521–531, Published online 10 December 2012 in Wiley Online Library (wileyonlinelibrary.com), DOI: 10.1002/per.1893

Lipman-Blumen, J., 2005, *The Allure of Toxic Leaders: Why We Follow Destructive Bosses and Corrupt Politicians: And How We Can Survive Them*, Oxford: Oxford University Press.

Matheieu, C., Neumann, C. S., Hare, D. R., & Babiak, P., 2014, A Dark Side of Leadership: Corporate Psychopathy and Its Influence on Employee Well-Being and Job Satisfaction. *Personality and Individual Differences*, 59, 83–88.

Paulhus, D. L. & Williams, K. M., 2002, The Dark Triad of Personality: Narcissism, Machiavellianism, and Psychopathy. *Journal of Research in Personality*, 36, 556–563.

Schyns, B. & Schilling, J., 2013, How Bad Are the Effects of Bad Leaders? A Meta-Analysis of Destructive Leadership and Its Outcomes. *The Leadership Quaterly*, 24, 138–158.

Tepper, B. J., 2000, Consequences of Abusive Supervision, *Academy of Management Journal*, 43, 178–190, https://doi.org/10.2307/1556375

Appendix 3
Disruptive behaviours/situations

Managing team conflict/disruptive behaviours in teams

This module calls for excellent standards of professionalism (commitment, reliability, creativity, etc.) and the vast majority of students thrive as a result. Excellent collaboration and teamwork, then, are key factors in your success on this module and any possible risk to this through disruption must be identified, monitored and swiftly resolved.

To attain the required standard of performance, each student is expected to reflect on their teams' performance and identify influential patterns of behaviour (including that of self), no matter how small the part played is (see Table A3.1 for examples of disruptive behaviours/situations).

The university recognises that teamwork can be challenging. However, it is a pertinent skill also required in the wider world of work (beyond academia). This is one of the main reasons why the module provides an opportunity to develop teambuilding/teamwork skills. Communication, interpersonal skills, and running effective meetings, which also includes managing attendance, are examples of such (transferable) skills. Others are task allocation and monitoring progress, e.g. dealing with lack of contribution and maintaining standards. To assist with managing the team formation process, I encourage each team to develop and use their Team Learning Contract, Peer Assessment Document, and a Team Résumé, as well as apply the necessary theories (such as Tuckman's Team Building/Performance Model and Belbin's Team Roles Model). Students must also gather evidence of efforts that they have made to manage the team situations as they occur. Where the problems persist, I must be informed sooner rather than later; at which point I will step in to *facilitate* the process. I will require evidence of incidents and efforts made to ameliorate the problem.

Table A3.1 Disruptive Behaviours/Situations

Typically Disruption May Occur When, for Example:		*Summary of Most Disruptive Behaviour Occurs When:*
Communication is poor between team members (including inactive listening)	Warning/s to team members about their disruption is/are ignored	*Team members are disrespected.*
Participation is poor during team meetings or other team learning events	Team members feels that they are being taken advantage of/their helpfulness is being taken for granted	*Team members are treated unfairly.*
Members of the team are late or do not attend scheduled meetings/team learning events	There is minimal or no contribution to coursework, team learning events and/or during other team meetings	*Team members are persistent in negative behaviours/refuse to learn and make amendments.*
Team members are not contactable/not responding to messages from peers when deemed absolutely necessary	When the contribution is shoddy	
Team members are being dishonest (remember unnecessary silence can also mean agreement)	Contracts (oral or written) are breached	

Appendix 4
Reflection colouring book

Test how colouring aids your IL and RL mindfulness/reflection and share your experience with us though by email: Team1.LJJM@irlcd.com.

Image A4.1

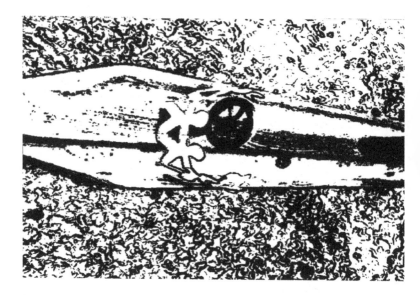

Image A4.2

Image A4.3

Image A4.4

Image A4.5

Index

Note: Page numbers in *italics* indicate figures; page numbers in **bold** indicate tables.

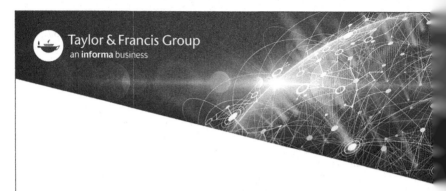

Printed in the United States
by Baker & Taylor Publisher Services